Planning Educational
Facilities

THE LIBRARY OF EDUCATION

A Project of The Center for Applied Research in Education, Inc.

G. R. Gottschalk, Director

Categories of Coverage

I	II	III
Curriculum and Teaching	Administration, Organization, and Finance	Psychology for Educators

IV	V	VI
History, Philosophy, and Social Foundations	Professional Skills	Educational Institutions

Planning Educational Facilities

DONALD J. LEU

Professor of Education
Michigan State University

The Center for Applied Research in Education, Inc.
New York

Library of Congress
Catalog Card No.: 65–14301

PRINTED IN THE UNITED STATES OF AMERICA

Foreword

Planning Educational Facilities provides a timely treatment of this complex subject. The materials included have been developed through years of direct involvement in school districts ranging in size from small rural schools to building programs located in our largest metropolitan cities. Educational leaders, boards of education, school architects, and involved lay citizens will find this book most helpful in the planning of their school buildings.

School building planning and construction represents a multi-billion dollar annual investment in the United States. Rapid and substantial changes are the predominant characteristics of these new schools. The author's analysis of emerging curriculum changes and their direct effect on school buildings makes this book a valuable contribution to the literature of school administration.

A substantial portion of the book is directed to the specifics of planning. Modernization of obsolete school buildings, estimating future enrollments, developing educational specifications, selecting the school architect, and financing the building program receive careful attention. Planning for the future appears to be a repetitive theme throughout the publication.

Most school administrators and lay citizens have had limited experience in the planning of educational facilities. Yet, careful planning will pay large educational dividends during the half-century life span of the school plant. School buildings have a direct effect on the school curriculum. This book should serve as a valuable aid in the continuing task of improving education.

RICHARD L. FEATHERSTONE
Assistant Dean, College of Education
Michigan State University

Planning Educational Facilities

Donald J. Leu

Planning Educational Facilities is a very fine book, written on a topic which, while very important to education, is rarely discussed in such a comprehensive, knowledgeable manner. Drawing upon a rich background of experience in the planning and constructing of educational facilities, Dr. Leu has produced a volume which is informative as well as highly readable.

The book opens on a discussion of early school buildings, moves quickly to a presentation of how to determine school building needs, how to plan a building, to modernize a building, and then how to finance the capital outlay. The book concludes with a look into the future, and the whole argument is summarized with a case which describes in concrete terms the concepts and generalizations discussed earlier.

Not only does this volume present what might be called "principles of educational facilities," but it also comes down to fundamentals in its discussion of such matters as estimating school enrollments or evaluating existing educational facilities. Since each topic is dealt with in specifics, it might well be said that this is a practical book on a practical subject. The book takes the reader step-by-step from the inception of the idea that a building is needed to the opening of the building. At the same time, the reader does not flounder in minutiae since all of the detail is constrained within a carefully developed frame of reference.

The author, Dr. Donald J. Leu, is an international consultant on the planning and construction of educational facilities. He holds the rank of Professor of Education at the College of Education, Michigan State University.

DANIEL E. GRIFFITHS
Content Editor

Contents

Planning Educational
Facilities

CHAPTER I

Historical Development of
Educational Facilities

School buildings are almost as old as civilization. A cave and the surrounding terrain probably served as the first one-room schoolhouse where father taught son the techniques of survival and food procurement and mother instructed daughter in the homemaking techniques of that era. The curriculum in those days featured "basic education," and the schoolhouse-cave was selected for this purpose. Over the years, the schoolhouse was modernized to serve its expanding curriculum. However, log cabins, sod huts, and other inadequate one-room schools were being used here in America up to and including the twentieth century. In fact, a surprising number of one-room schools, featuring pot-bellied stoves, leaking roofs, and outdoor plumbing and water supply are still in use in parts of our nation.

Dramatic changes in our society have rendered obsolete these older schoolhouses. Yet, recent trends in schoolhouse design are attempting to retain and recapture some of the unique advantages of these archaic schools of a bygone era. Close and personal contact between teacher and child, individualized instruction, "little-schools," and independent study are, for example, concepts being adapted to today's larger and more comprehensive schools.

School building construction has become a multi-billion dollar business in the United States. The value of our existing school plants is roughly estimated to be four times the assets of our nation's largest corporation.[1] Forty-two million public school children receive their formal education in these buildings. In 1963 the school enrollment increased by approximately one and a half million pupils. Nearly one-fourth of the people of the United States spend their working days in public, private, or parochial school buildings. The

[1] *The Cost of a Schoolhouse* (New York: The Educational Facilities Laboratories, Inc., 1960), p. 1.

1

issue of what to build, when to build, and how to build the school building affects the typical citizen in two sensitive areas—his purse and his child. School buildings represent a major commitment of tax dollars and have a direct impact on the quantity and quality of education.

Investment in School Buildings

Citizens of our nation are investing in excess of three billion dollars per year in providing educational facilities for their children and youth. A number of factors have contributed to this tremendous school building program. The depression years of the 1930's rendered it financially difficult for many school districts to provide needed new facilities or to retire existing obsolete school buildings. World War II, following on the heels of the depression years, made it virtually impossible to secure building materials and skilled labor for nonmilitary purposes. The number of births in the United States mushroomed from 2.6 million in 1940 to 4.0 million in 1953.[2] This high birth rate has continued into the 1960's. During the past half-century the population has almost doubled from 91 million residents in 1910 to over 179 million in 1960. Increased population mobility has shifted large segments of the population from rural farms and villages to our congested metropolitan complexes. These factors have continued the critical shortage of adequate educational facilities.

Early School Buildings

The rural one-room school was the typical school building during the early years of the nineteenth century. Frequently it served the varied purposes of teacher's home, schoolhouse, and community center. Usually these school buildings were dark, dirty, unhealthy, and poorly suited to the purposes of education. Pupils of all ages were crowded together on fixed benches and were instructed by teachers of varying levels of preparation. However, many of today's citizens still retain fond memories of these early schools.

As America changed from a rural to an urban society, our school buildings grew larger and more complex. The graded elementary school emerged. The Quincy Grammar School constructed in Bos-

---

[2] United States Bureau of the Census, *Statistical Abstract of the United States* (Washington, D.C.: Government Printing Office, 1959), p. 11.

ton in 1848 was a prototype of many schools throughout the land. The building consisted of twelve classrooms, an assembly hall, and a principal's office. The school was located on a site of less than one acre and consisted of four stories, basement, and attic. The assembly hall, located on the fourth floor, was large enough to hold the entire student body of 660 students. Each of the remaining box-like floors was divided into four classrooms and a central corridor. Fifty-five students, in fixed individual seats, were squeezed into each classroom. The toilet rooms and heating plant were located in the basement of the school. It is interesting to note that this school building, built over a century ago, is still in use today.

The American public high school followed the Kalamazoo court decision of 1874. (This court decision established the right of local school districts to operate high schools at public expense.) Cupolas, parapet walls, high ceilings, excessive ornamentation, and central fan heating systems were characteristic of these early secondary schools. As society increased in complexity, the comprehensive high school emerged. The original school building received additions, consisting largely of shops, homemaking rooms, commercial rooms, and music, physical education, and science facilities. The "bearing wall" construction of this period made it exceedingly difficult to make major changes in the interior of the existing school buildings. Large city schools began constructing separate buildings for vocational and commercial training of some of their secondary school students.

The depression of 1930 resulted in an economy wave throughout the public sector of our society. The few school buildings constructed were stripped of wasteful ornamentation and became boxes with windows. In respect to exterior design, it became difficult to distinguish between prisons, school buildings, and post offices. The federal government supported the construction of most public school buildings built during this depression period.

The Educational Facilities Laboratories calls attention to some unique exceptions to the general pattern of early school building design:

> There were notable exceptions to these monumental buildings with their impressive entries and halls and their depressing rooms. Frank Lloyd Wright's Hillsdale Home School in Spring Green, Wisconsin, done at the turn of the century, and Dwight Perkins' Carl

Schurz High School in Chicago in 1910 were two that pointed the way toward open planning on a scale more appropriate to the younger generation, and a freedom from the dictates of historical eclecticism. But exceptions were rare until just before the Second World War when an explosion of architectural creativity hit the schoolhouse.

Heralding the explosion was Neutra's work in California in the 1930's. 1940 saw the construction of the Crow Island School in Winnetka, Illinois—a schoolhouse that called considerable attention to its new forms and ideas. Saarinen and Swanson, Perkins and Will, were associated architects. Their building influenced not only school architecture as architecture, but also the relation of plant to program. It was the result, as Lawrence B. Perkins has written, "of months of study on the part of teachers, architects and administrators."[3]

Recent Trends

Most school buildings constructed a decade or two ago are massive, multi-story structures with "egg-crate" classrooms along both sides of a central corridor. These buildings have a severe, institutional look and a rugged, enduring quality. Roof lines are flat, building lines are straight, and window area is abundant. Myriad, and sometimes grotesque, attempts were made to let large quantities of daylight into the classroom, and "glassblock" window areas were common. Various design attempts were made to control the resultant glare and heat gain. Effective use of electronic and audiovisual teaching aids was difficult. Soon school districts were constructing larger school buildings to house the increasing enrollment located in high-density population centers and in reorganized rural school districts.

The current decade has witnessed dramatic changes in school building design. These educational and architectural changes have paralleled the rapid changes taking place in our society. Architects, educators, and lay citizens have teamed together in the reshaping of American school buildings.

The "finger plan" became common in the early part of this period. It provided a way of breaking down large massive units into smaller units to relieve congestion and noise and to bring outside light into the classroom. The finger plan had the added advantage

[3] *The Cost of a Schoolhouse, op. cit.,* p. 31.

of making expansion of buildings easy as enrollment increased. "Campus-type" buildings in which clusters of classrooms or "little-schools" scattered over the site were also frequently designed. These buildings adapted easily into the existing terrain, were not unusually expensive, and could lend themselves to rapid expansion or change. Compact "little-schools," which decentralize large groups of students, are again becoming more common. Exterior walls are shorter, exterior glass is reduced, and interior space is fluid and flexible in most modern designs.

Relating design to learning theory. Recent school buildings reflect an increasing concern with the environmental effects of the physical space on teaching and learning. School buildings are being scaled to the ages, interests, and behavioral traits of children. Classroom interiors are finished in stimulating colors and utilize natural wood, exposed brick, and other attractive materials. In attempts to create a quiet and pleasing total environment, architects are developing and enhancing the natural beauty of rolling, wooded sites.

Sound control, quality lighting, and controlled thermal environment are receiving increasing attention. Air conditioning is becoming common. Carpeting for floors is sometimes used. Beauty is being emphasized through simplicity of design, careful use of colors, and a commitment to "aesthetic surprises" throughout the building. The inherent worth, dignity, and individuality of each student receives architectural concern. Differentiation of spaces for students of various age groups, differing abilities, and interests are provided. The rigidity and stiffness so familiar in older classrooms has given way to informal and nonthreatening spaces. In short, many architects are attempting to design a physical environment that will not only contribute to existing theories of learning, but also assimilate educational changes.

Specialized facilities. As the instructional program broadens and pupils and teachers use a wider range of equipment and materials, there is more need for larger rooms, increased storage space, greater flexibility, and furniture and equipment that is easily movable. Built-in equipment is being replaced by deployable units. A sink, an art area, science space, and specialized equipment are becoming major parts of the elementary classroom. Teacher-planning areas, social areas for students, and independent study carrels are being provided. The library is being replaced by a broadened concept of the "instructional materials center," with an increased amount of the building resembling library-like space.

Guidance and counseling areas are being expanded and removed from the administrative suite. A larger amount of the building area is being used for a wide variety of mechanical aids (language laboratories, TV, programmed learning, etc.). It should be noted that an increasing percentage of the construction budget is being diverted from construction materials to specialized equipment.[4]

The Cost of School Buildings

Continuing pressure has been exerted on educators and architects to stretch the school building dollar. The reduction or elimination of corridors and basement spaces has been one result of this economy drive. Modular construction, repetitive framing, and the use of new construction techniques and materials have resulted in considerable cost reductions. School architects are utilizing careful design techniques to achieve true economy without sacrifices in educational adequacy or maintenance costs. For example, one large city reduced the construction costs of their new school buildings by 8 per cent during a five-year period. Over this same period of time the Building Cost Index for this city rose by 19 per cent.[5] This cost reduction, involving twenty million dollars of new construction, was accomplished without a reduction in the educational adequacy of the school buildings.

A study by the American Association of School Administrators revealed that during a twenty-year period (1937–1956) the following national increases occurred in construction costs:

1. General construction costs increased 275 per cent.
2. Medium-priced brick residences increased 225 per cent.
3. All buildings increased 210 per cent.
4. School buildings increased 150 per cent.[6]

---

[4] The author has drawn from the annual slide presentations on school building design developed each year by The American Association of School Administrators. The 1963 slide report entitled *A Decade of Progress in School Building Construction* has been heavily utilized in the analysis of recent trends.

[5] Donald J. Leu and John J. McNicholas, *Five Years of Progress* (East Lansing, Michigan: College of Education, Michigan State University, 1960), p. 8.

[6] *Stretching the School Building Dollar* (Washington, D.C.: The American Association of School Administrators, 1957), p. 2.

During this same period the following changes occurred in those factors affecting the cost of school buildings:

1. Common labor increased 330 per cent.
2. Skilled labor increased 220 per cent.
3. Structural steel increased 215 per cent.
4. Materials and components for construction increased 200 per cent.[7]

Obviously, school buildings are being constructed with economy in cost as an important goal. It is interesting to ask those individuals who are charging the schools with high construction costs to compare school building costs with the costs of other types of construction. The writer recently completed a study of comparative square foot costs with the following results:

Types of Construction	Per Square Foot
Bank	$34.00
Office Building	33.00
Hospital	26.00
Prison	24.00
School	16.00
Typical brick house	15.00[8]

Economy should be properly defined as achieving the greatest educational return for each tax dollar invested. It should not be confused with cheapness, high maintenance costs, or omission of needed educational spaces and equipment. During the past decade American school buildings have made excellent progress towards achieving true economy.

---

[7] *Ibid.*, p. 3.

[8] Donald J. Leu and John J. McNicholas, *A Look at Your School Buildings* (East Lansing, Michigan: College of Education, Michigan State University, 1960), pp. 93–94.

CHAPTER II

Determining
Local School Building Needs

Planning of educational facilities may be divided into two rather distinct phases: the planning *for* future school building needs and the planning *of* individual school buildings. This chapter directs itself to the planning for future school building needs.

School districts, throughout the nation, are facing numerous problems associated with obsolete educational facilities, mushrooming school enrollments, and increasing mobility of population. The problem has recently been further complicated by the introduction of complex socioeconomic factors as an important issue in the location and utilization of educational facilities. For example, the school's racial characteristics, resulting from the specific location of a school site, is a new issue confronting the educational planner.

In the past, school plant studies have frequently consisted of estimating school enrollments, computing building capacity, subtracting the capacity from the estimated enrollment, and, on the basis of these minimal data, developing recommendations for a building program. Occasionally, partial glances were taken at available financial resources. In most instances, the survey was conducted in relative secrecy with selected citizens called in prior to the bond issue to help sell the program to the voters. Little or no attention was given to existing or desired educational programs, the changing community, or the educational understanding and aspirations of the local citizens. Sometimes an outside "expert" was called in for a few days to give quick answers to complex problems or to "rubber stamp" preconceived solutions. Fortunately these types of studies are rapidly disappearing. Experience has shown that the changing understanding and aspirations of people who are involved or acquainted with the workings of the school plant study have more far-reaching implications for school improvement than the mere publication of a printed survey report.

8

Most recent school building surveys have at least three major objectives:

1. To develop a recommended long-term school building program.
2. To formulate recommended first steps in achieving the long-term program.
3. To create community understanding of and desire for improved educational programs.

One caution needs attention prior to launching a study of local school building needs. Many school districts throughout the United States are initiating or completing studies of school plant needs when their primary problems are actually those of school district reorganization. Prior to initiating a school plant study, school officials should ask these questions about the organization of their school district:

1. Does the existing school district organization permit a complete and efficient educational program for all the children (grades Kindergarten–12 or Kindergarten–14) in the service area?
2. Do existing school district lines follow logical service, geographical, and community boundaries?
3. Are there sufficient local financial resources to support a quality educational program?

Unless school officials can answer these questions affirmatively, the primary problem may be one of school district reorganization.

Organizing for a School Plant Study

A school plant study is a thoughtful undertaking enabling local citizens to plan for one portion of their over-all community needs— future school facilities. Six basic questions are involved:

1. What kinds of educational programs and facilities do we have now?
2. What kinds of educational programs and facilities do we desire?
3. What new educational facilities are needed to achieve our goals?
4. Where should the new educational facilities be located?
5. How much will the proposed school plant program cost?
6. How can the proposed school plant program be financed?

There are a number of accepted methods of conducting a school plant study. The survey completed by the Superintendent of Schools and his administrative staff is the most common type of study. The outside "expert" or team study is another. Citizen-type surveys have become increasingly common. During recent years, a type of survey utilizing many of the human resources available in and to the school district under the over-all direction of the Superintendent of Schools has been gaining in use.

All of these methods of studying school plant needs have had varying degrees of success; no one method is always best. However, the one-man survey and the outside "expert" approach to school plant problems have been rapidly diminishing in use and value.

A study of school plant needs usually consists of ten different phases:

1. Identifying the problem.
2. Outlining and delimiting the scope of the study.
3. Organizing the human resources to be utilized.
4. Gathering facts and information.
5. Analyzing and evaluating data.
6. Developing tentative recommendations.
7. Refining, coordinating, and modifying the tentative recommendations in cooperation with other community planning agencies.
8. Reporting the findings and recommendations.
9. Taking action on the survey recommendations.
10. Reviewing and revising the recommendations periodically.

Studies of school plant needs should be sponsored by the legally constituted Board of Education. The school board should understand and endorse the organization for the study, the scope of the project, and the personnel to be involved. The Superintendent of Schools should be the key person in the study, exerting leadership and direction to the entire study enterprise.

Figure 1 illustrates one method of organizing for a school plant study. It may be easily adapted by school districts ranging in size from small rural schools to large metropolitan school systems.[1]

A school building survey normally includes the broad areas of: (1) the school-community, (2) school enrollments, (3) educational program, and (4) school buildings.

The following checklist has been developed by the author to serve as a guide for conducting a school plant study. The list is not definitive and should be modified to serve individual school districts.

---

[1] Donald J. Leu and John L. Forbes, *What is Involved in Conducting a School Plant Study?* (East Lansing, Michigan: College of Education, Michigan State University, 1956), p. 6.

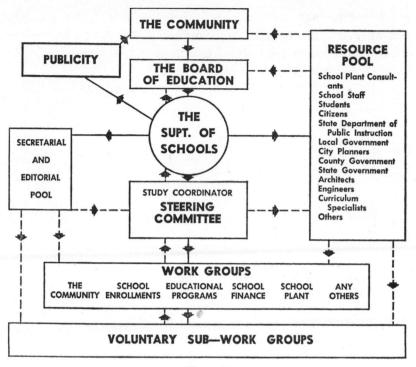

Figure 1.

The school-community

(Suggested reference material: census data, zoning maps, traffic artery maps, housing maps)

1. What are the characteristics of the existing population?
2. What is the existing population?
3. What is the estimated future population?
4. What is the existing zoning?
5. What zoning changes are proposed or needed?
6. Is there a master plan for developing our community?
7. How much land is available for residential development?
8. How many residential building permits were issued during the last few years?
9. What land has been plotted?
10. What residential buildings are planned by building developers?
11. Where are new and older houses located?
12. Where are the school district lines?
13. Where are the major traffic arteries?
14. Where are future traffic arteries to be located?

School Enrollments

(Suggested reference material: school census and school census cards, spot maps, etc.)

1. How many pre-school children are there?
2. How many students are enrolled in each grade of our schools?
3. What is the past history of enrollments?
4. Where do the children live?
5. How many nonresident pupils?
6. How many tuition pupils?
7. How many parochial and private school pupils?
8. What are the expansion plans of private and parochial schools?
9. What is the history of birth rates?
10. How many new houses are being built or planned?
11. How many children do these new homes have?
12. Which enrollment-estimating method should we use?
13. What percentage of the school census children will:
    a. enter kindergarten?
    b. continue in elementary school?
    c. enter secondary school?
    d. complete secondary school?
14. What is the estimate of future enrollments?
15. What are the assumptions of the estimate?

Educational Progam

1. What is the most desirable school organization for our school district? (K-6, 3, 3, or K-8, 9-12, etc.)
2. How large or small should our schools be?
3. How many children should be in each class?
4. What is the existing elementary school program?
5. What is the desired elementary school program?
6. What is the existing secondary school program?
7. How can it be improved?
8. What happens to our high school graduates?
9. How many students drop out of our schools?
10. Why do these students leave?
11. What provisions do we make for exceptional children?
    a. handicapped
    b. gifted
    c. retarded
12. To what extent will the community use our schools?

School Buildings

1. How adequate is each building in terms of:
   a. age
   b. size of site

    c. facilities (floor plan)
    d. educational adequacy (rating form)
    e. structural adequacy (rating form)
    f. pupil capacity
    g. pupil utilization
    h. estimated enrollment
2. What is the total capacity of all school buildings?
3. What is the total utilization of all school buildings?
4. How safe are the school buildings?
5. What modernization is needed?

Recommendations

1. What is happening in the community that affects the schools?
2. What is the school's role in a changing community?
3. What is the desired educational program?
4. How adequate is the existing school plant?
5. What modernization is needed?
6. What new facilities are needed?
7. What are the recommended steps in the proposed building program?
8. How much will it cost?
9. How should it be financed?
10. How will it affect our tax rates?
11. What are the next steps in educational planning?
12. Who should be involved?
13. How should they be involved?

School-Community Planning

The planning and locating of educational facilities should be carefully coordinated with other public and private planning agencies. Schools, parks, libraries, churches, and social service agencies serve the same population with overlapping functions. For example, it is poor planning to locate a new school site without careful attention to the future location of new parks, highways, urban renewal projects, or industrial expansion. These illustrations are a few examples of the increasing need for coordinated school-community planning. The city and/or metropolitan planning agency is the single most important unit able to aid the school building planner.

School districts must consider and understand the complex educational implications resulting from the rapid socioeconomic-political changes presently taking place in our metropolitan and rural areas. Much of the data needed for analysis of the community may be readily acquired from the various planning agencies and from the data compiled by the United States Bureau of the Census.

Census data. Census data provides valuable information directly related to the long-term planning of education facilities. For example, it would seem obvious that a community's ability to provide and support education would be impacted by the comparative income of its citizenry. The following table compares the median family income of two central cities with their surrounding metropolitan neighbors. This table clearly indicates that the citizens of the central cities have comparatively less individual income with which to support a quality educational program and facilities.

TABLE 1

MEDIAN FAMILY INCOME
METROPOLITAN MINNEAPOLIS *

Community	Median Family Income
Edina	$12,082
Minnetonka	8,180
St. Louis Park	7,808
Richfield	7,721
Bloomington	7,201
Hennepin County (Average)	6,954
St. Paul	6,543
Minneapolis	6,401

* Source: United States Bureau of the Census, *U.S. Census of Population and Housing: 1960* (Washington, D.C.: The Bureau, 1960).

Additional related tables and charts may be easily developed from available census data. These visual illustrations aid the professional planner and lay citizen in understanding his changing school-community. The following basic table titles are suggested for developing descriptive tables in the School-Community section of a school building study:

1. Median School Years completed by Persons Twenty-five Years Old and Older.
2. Median Age.
3. Negro Population Concentrations by Census Tracts.
4. Labor Force Characteristics.
5. Characteristics of the Nonwhite Population.
6. Percentage of Housing Units Occupied by Renters and Owners.

Land utilization and zoning. Zoning is a method of dividing an area into zones or districts, and regulating land uses and related matters within such areas. It has a direct effect on the health, safety, comfort, and convenience of all the people in an area because it impinges upon traffic and parking, civic congestion, slum prevention, sewers, water supply, schools, parks, playgrounds, fire prevention, general community and neighborhood appearance, municipal revenues and expenditures, and property values. Zoning has a considerable effect upon the rate of population growth. In terms of planning, zoning is a device to implement the land use plan.

School planners have a vital stake in the type of future zoning and the enforcement of existing zoning ordinances. School districts located in rapidly growing metropolitan areas are most directly affected by zoning and land use plans. Actually the quality and quantity of future educational needs are directly related to zoning and land utilization. Poor zoning normally results in an inadequate financial base for support of education, industrial areas overlapping residential neighborhoods, and the lack of adequate, properly located school sites. The school should play an active partnership role in the development of adequate zoning ordinances. Some school districts are represented on planning commission policy-making boards with an increasing number of school districts moving towards a joint appointment on the planning commission's technical staff. It is imperative that the school district recognize that any change in zoning regulations can alter its planning significantly. For this reason, continued close cooperation and consultation with the appropriate municipal planning agencies is absolutely necessary.

Traffic arteries. Any long-range building program must take into careful consideration traffic routes (actual and potential) of freeways, highways, and streets within a school district. The potential hazards of such thoroughfares are quite apparent to all; not so obvious to the lay observer, however, is the possible isolation of a particular section of a school attendance area due to new highway construction. Present and future traffic conditions as they relate to the safe movement of children from their homes to school and back need our attention. The effect of a new traffic pattern on community development is crucial. Roadways carrying heavy or fast traffic directly affect the location of new school buildings as well as any expansion or modernization plans on existing sites. These routes may preclude needed site expansion. Heavily trafficked streets and highways, planned without adequate safety features and pedestrian conveniences, present serious hazards for school children.

A map illustrating the location of existing and future traffic routes is a useful planning tool. A second map showing the relative traffic densities of existing streets will aid in planning the location of future school facilities. Unfortunately, many school buildings are facing premature obsolescence by the location of new freeways which disregard the location of the neighborhood school. Schools are being isolated from their service areas by the lack of coordinated planning and the apparent lack of adequate controls over highway planners. In fact, all the careful long-range planning of schools, parks, and neighborhoods can be made worthless by the indiscriminate location of a new interstate freeway system. Coordinated planning is the only realistic solution to this recent problem.

Urban redevelopment. A recent phenomenon to the American scene affecting the need for school buildings, their location, and their size is the emergence of urban redevelopment projects. The old concept that a city must decay, wear out, and be abandoned to blight has now been replaced by the knowledge that areas can be redeveloped and maintained. The tool is urban renewal. Renewal can be applied in some appropriate manner to every part of a metropolitan area and all land uses. As areas begin to deteriorate, they can be rehabilitated to an acceptable standard. Eventually the age and obsolescence of structures may require that they be cleared and redeveloped.

Urban redevelopment usually includes three operations: (1) clearance and renewal of slums, (2) rehabilitation of rundown but sound structures, and (3) conservation of good structures. These operations, typically, are carried out on the basis of designated project areas rather than treatment of individual structures.

All uses—manufacturing, business, residential, and public—are included as both subjects and beneficiaries of renewal action. While housing receives the most attention, it is not unique in its claim to renewal. Structural and functional obsolescence, rising standards, increased traffic and parking requirements, and changing production methods cause blight in many nonresidential areas. Since the tax base of most cities is largely based on commercial and industrial activity, protection and preservation of the existing economic base is a critical factor and is usually given high priority in the future scheduling of projects.

The degree to which redevelopment will succeed is greatly affected by the actions of many groups. The most effective modus operandi is through the close relationship of renewal to the comprehensive city plan. The operation of many municipal departments and private agencies affect redevelopment. If the plan is to succeed, the most effective approach is one of complete understanding and close cooperation among affected groups. School building planning is a vital and interrelated portion of urban renewal. One urban renewal project may dramatically increase or decrease the need for school facilities.

Obviously, there are limitations to urban redevelopment. One of the most crucial and unpredictable is finance. The availability of federal and municipal incomes is always uncertain, subject to the whims and vagaries of changing political pressures. Relocation of displaced families and individuals is a most important limitation, and this problem can be compounded greatly when extensive demolition is being effected simultaneously by freeway authorities.

Federal aid for project expenditures is presently available for redevelopment with the federal government paying two-thirds and the city paying the remaining one-third. It is significant to note that the cost of school buildings may be utilized as a portion of the city's share. Federal mortgage insurance is available for financing rehabilitation of residential structures and construction of new dwellings. The National Housing Act also provides mortgage insurance for assistance in relocating families from urban renewal areas or those displaced as a result of government action.

It is obvious to even the casual observer that intelligent school plant planning should not be limited by the fixed boundaries of the redevelopment area and that it should consider the implications of redevelopment for contiguous areas as well. Urban planning, like educational planning, cannot be accomplished in a vacuum. The involvement of other public agencies such as the school board is necessary and desirable.

Population estimates. Accurate estimates of future school enrollments are of prime importance in planning educational facilities. School enrollments constitute a portion of the total population. Therefore, any analysis of a school-community should include a careful review of existing population estimates.

Seldom in the history of the United States has the need for an accurate estimation of population been greater than at the present time. Never before has such estimation been more difficult, for the forces determining population in a given locality have never before assumed the complexity, the scale, or the variability of those now at work on the American scene. More specifically, efforts to estimate population today must, among other things, reckon with great population and community changes. These changes among the population factors include unprecedented mobility, increased concentrations of population in metropolitan areas, accelerating decentralizing of the "core" city, great waves of in-migrant people of diverse race and cultural background, and rapidly changing age characteristics. Simultaneously, kaleidoscopic community changes are under way, including changes in pattern of densities of land use arising from urban renewal programs, public housing projects, federal and local highway construction, and ever-increasing traffic flows. Furthermore, the problem of estimating school population for specific local educational purposes is not made easier by the differential rates of expansion of public, private, and parochial schools, or by the increasing need to replace obsolescent school structures, even while grappling with problems of growth and mobility.

Efforts to estimate population must necessarily take into account the effect of each of the variables mentioned previously. In general, the larger the area for which the estimate is made, the more accurate it is likely to be. Table 2 indicates a typical population pattern for a metropolitan area: growth of the suburbs and a decline in population of the central city. It is interesting to note that while our large central cities lost population during the past decade, they gained in school enrollment. This is explained to a great extent by the large

TABLE 2

POPULATION TRENDS IN
HENNEPIN COUNTY COMMUNITIES
1950–1960 *

Community	1950	1960	Increase	Per Cent
Edina	9,774	28,501	18,757	192.5
Golden Valley	5,551	14,559	9,008	162.3
Richfield	17,502	42,523	25,021	143.0
St. Louis Park	22,644	43,310	20,666	91.3
Hopkins	7,595	11,370	3,775	49.7
Robbinsdale	11,289	16,381	5,092	45.1
Minneapolis	521,718	482,872	−38,846	−7.4
Hennepin County	676,718	842,854	166,375	24.6

Source: United States Bureau of the Census. *United States Census of Population and Housing: 1960.* Number of Inhabitants—Minnesota.

scale migration of low income families to the central city. These low income families are typically public school adherents and have a higher percentage of school-age children than the families they have replaced. Thus the problems of planning educational facilities are further increased.

Estimating School Enrollments

Any long-range plan for a local school district must be based on the number of students who are to be educated. School buildings are designed to provide an educational program for a specified number of students. Accurate estimates of future enrollments are a difficult but necessary part of any study of future school building needs.

Unfortunately, there is no single best method of projecting future school enrollments. Local conditions of growth, along with the availability of basic data, should dictate the specific method to be utilized. The most common methods currently employed to estimate future school enrollments are: (1) percentage of survival, (2) percentage of population, (3) percentage of census, (4) housing population analysis, and (5) methods combining two or more of the previous methods in adjusting the final estimates. The method used by the estimator along with the completeness and appropriateness of his raw data will condition the accuracy of his estimate. More important, however, than his data or methodology is the experienced judgment utilized by the enrollment estimator in identifying and utilizing the many variables determining actual future enrollments. The statement of his basic assumptions relating to these variables will make it readily apparent when the estimate has outlived its usefulness and needs revision.

It is relatively easy to make accurate estimates of the total school district's enrollment for a short period of time. However, school buildings are planned for approximately 50 years of life and estimates must be made for each school building's attendance area. The changing of one uncontrollable variable may make any estimate quickly obsolete. For example, a modification in zoning by a city agency may quickly change an existing area's population potential. The relocation of a planned high-rise low income apartment complex has embarrassed former prophets. Obviously, coordinated and controlled long-term planning is a necessary prerequisite to accurate estimates of school enrollment.

Percentage of survival technique.   The following description developed by the Educational Facilities Laboratories succinctly explains the percentage of survival technique. Among these more refined forecasting methods, the simplest and perhaps the most widely used has been the "percentage of survival technique."

The first step in this procedure is to estimate future enrollments by computing the estimated size of each grade for the next immediate year from the size of the present year's next lower grade. Of the children in any grade, a certain percentage "survive" to enter the next higher grade the following year. This percentage may be more or less than 100 per cent, depending primarily on population changes but also somewhat on the promotion policy of the school system. In a similar fashion, some percentage of this new grade group "survives" again in each subsequent year as it advances to the next higher grade.

By computing an average of what this percentage of grade-to-grade survival has been for, say, the past five years, it becomes possible to advance the present total school enrollment year by year, each time dropping the last grade and adding a new first-grade group. The size of this new yearly first grade is also estimated by using a "survival" ration, again based on past experience but this time on the number of births in relation to those entering the first grade. Table 3 illustrates this method.

This method of forecasting is neat and orderly, but because of its very neatness may not always do the job. It is a technique which should be used carefully and with an awareness of its weakness—a tendency to oversimplify the picture. It takes all of the numerous factors which more or less independently affect school enrollments and welds them into one single factor. It says that in this community we feel confident that what has been happening in the past is continuing pretty much as it has been, or that, if there are changes they are tending to cancel each other out, leaving the net balance of conditions about the way it was. In view of the quantity and quality of the population movement taking place in America, this is often a dangerous assumption. Some communities have miscalculated in using this technique because of the failure to take into account the sudden in-migration or out-migration from church-related schools.[2]

---

[2] *The Cost of a Schoolhouse* (New York: The Educational Facilities Laboratories, Inc., 1960), pp. 52–53.

An example of a single class is used in the following "percentage of survival" table to show how class size can be estimated from year to year for a six-year period.

TABLE 3

ESTIMATING SCHOOL ENROLLMENTS

Survival Ratios ..	(1.2)	(.88)	(1.1)	(1.0)	(1.2)	(1.0)	(.97)	
Grade	Kdg	1st	2nd	3rd	4th	5th	6th	Year
(Actual)	101	97	85	92	84	73	64	1960
(Estimated)								
90 *	108							1961
		95						1962
			105					1963
				105				1964
					126			1965
						126		1966

* This figure of 90 children represents the births to residents of the previous five-year period: 1956. Ninety children born in 1956 will be of Kindergarten age in 1961.

Percentage of census technique.   Several states and numerous school districts conduct an annual census of their total population or their school-age population. This annual census is usually taken during the spring or summer months. Some school districts will conduct this census of the total population as a part of a comprehensive school building study in anticipation of a major school building expansion program. This census information, when available, provides a valuable source of data for the enrollment estimator. Professional educational facility planners have found that enrollment projections based on accurate school census data is the soundest method of estimating future school enrollments.

Basically, the percentage of census technique projects school population by ages rather than by enrollments. It utilizes the same projection method as the percentage of survival technique. Specific school enrollment estimates are completed by translating school-age population to school enrollments on the basis of past experience ratios. This experience ratio is frequently adjusted to anticipate any variations in public, private, or parochial school enrollment policies. For example, the planned construction of a new parochial high school in a relatively stable community would reduce the percentage of high school students attending the public schools.

Percentage of population technique. The percentage of population technique is most useful in making long-range estimates of enrollments. It is generally used in dealing with school groups rather than individual grade groupings. Basically, this technique relates school enrollments to a percentage of the total population. It is useful in checking an estimate made by the use of other enrollment projection methods.

The accuracy of this method is largely dependent upon the accuracy of the population estimate from which it is derived. Significant changes within the socioeconomic-age characteristics of the total population will increase the difficulties in establishing valid percentages of school population. The following table clearly illustrates the percentage of population technique.

TABLE 4

PUBLIC SCHOOL ENROLLMENTS, 1940 TO 1960 *
WITH ESTIMATES TO 1980

		ACTUAL			POTENTIAL	
	1930	*1940*	*1950*	*1960*	*1970*	*1980*
Kindergarten	6,910	5,017	6,171	7,333	7,905	7,125
Per cent	(1.5)	(1.0)	(1.2)	(1.5)	(1.7)	(1.5)
Grades 1-6	40,869	29,687	30,784	32,113	33,480	33,725
Per cent	(8.8)	(6.0)	(5.9)	(6.7)	(7.2)	(7.1)
Grades 7-9	18,666	17,580	12,661	15,905	15,810	16,625
Per cent	(4.0)	(3.6)	(2.4)	(3.3)	(3.4)	(3.5)
Grades 10-12	12,467	17,284	10,763	12,605	11,625	13,775
Per cent	(2.7)	(3.5)	(2.1)	(2.6)	(2.5)	(2.9)
Subtotal	78,912	69,568	60,379	67,956	68,820	71,250
Per cent	(17.0)	(14.1)	(11.6)	(14.1)	(14.8)	(15.0)
Vocational High School	1,425	2,297	1,752	1,528	1,400	1,600
Special Education	1,353	1,458	1,120	1,599	2,000	2,500
Special Groups	4	38	3			
Total	81,694	73,361	63,254	71,083	72,220	75,350
Minneapolis Population	464,356	492,370	521,718	482,872	465,000	475,000

* Source: Donald J. Leu and John J. McNicholas, *Planning for the Future, Minneapolis Public Schools* (East Lansing, Michigan: Michigan State University, 1963), p. 160.

Housing population analysis. This technique is most useful in rapidly growing suburban areas facing a major population explosion resulting from large-scale housing developments. It assumes that the future homes are going to be similar in size, cost, and in the number and ages of school children to an existing recent housing development. Frequently this estimate is placed "piggyback" over an existing projection of enrollment. For example, if a large-scale housing development is being planned for 1,200 three- and four-bedroom homes with an average sale price of $21,000, and these homes are to be constructed and sold duing an eighteen-month period, how many children in each grade level will these new homes produce?

A census of families in a similar new housing development might reveal the following information which could be added to existing forecasts of enrollment:

TABLE 5

AGE DISTRIBUTION OF CHILDREN IN
250 NEW SINGLE FAMILY DWELLINGS

Age		Number in Public Schools	Number in Private or Parochial Schools	Total	Public School Children, per House, by School Divisions
UNDER	1	15	2	17	
	1	19	6	25	
	2	19	2	21	
	3	21	4	25	
	4	29	4	33	
	5	23	2	25	
	6	25	5	30	
	7	29	6	35	Grades K-6
	8	25	3	28	.78
	9	21	0	21	
	10	19	4	23	
	11	27	5	32	
	12	21	1	22	Grades 7–9
	13	15	2	17	.24
	14	19	3	22	
	15	19	4	23	Grades 10–12
	16	17	1	18	.20
	17	?1	2	13	
	18	10	0	10	Total
OVER	18	12	7	19	Grades K-12 1.22
TOTAL		396	63	459	

Reducing the margin of error. Any estimate of future enrollment in a school district or specific school attendance area is difficult to prepare since the actual number of children that may be in the schools at some future date is dependent upon a number of variables. Assuming the best method of estimating enrollments is utilized, and assuming that complete and accurate data are available, large errors in estimates are still possible. The experienced judgments of the estimator in identifying variables and adjusting his final estimate to compensate for the effect of these variables is the key to accurate estimates of future school enrollments. These variables include the following:

1. Future local birth rates
2. In-migration of families with public school-age children
3. Out-migration of families with public school-age children
4. Changing socioeconomic characteristics of the population
5. Changing school policies of attendance of pupils both in and outside of the district
6. Changes in attendance boundaries
7. The extent, rate, and characteristics of new dwelling units
8. Shifts of population
9. Urban renewal projects
10. New freeway systems
11. Economic conditions

The above list is not exhaustive; rather, it is illustrative of the potential for enrollment changes within a local school district. Enrollment estimates should be constantly reviewed and revised in light of any changes in the variables listed above.

Evaluating Existing
Educational Facilities

A logical starting point in the determination of any long-range school building program is a careful examination of existing school plant facilities in terms of their educational adequacy, capacity, and utilization. Each school building and site should be carefully evaluated by an experienced school plant specialist. On the basis of his evaluation, the educational adequacy, the desirable and overcrowded capacities, and the current utilization of each building may be determined. These school building facts may then be combined with estimates of future enrollments to aid in determining needed additional facilities to serve the future needs of the school district.

Educational adequacy. The comparative educational adequacy of a school building may be determined by utilizing a standard checklist or rating form designed to measure the educational strengths and weaknesses of the existing school buildings. All rating forms have the inherent weakness of reflecting the educational values of the individual developing the rating device. Their major advantage lies in their ability to carefully compare the individual school buildings through the use of a detailed rating form which applies the same criteria of adequacy to all the schools.

One frequently used rating form is the Linn-McCormick Rating Form for School Plants.[3] This rating form provides a detailed method of evaluating the following features of a school building:

1. Site
2. Building Structure
3. Heating and ventilating
4. Fire protection
5. Artificial illumination
6. Electric services
7. Toilets and water supply
8. Lockers and storage
9. Classrooms
10. General rooms
11. Administrative rooms
12. Special rooms

Consideration of both the individual scores and the total score for each building provides a basis upon which to appraise the adequacy of each plant for educational purposes. On this rating form, for example, a perfect school plant would receive a score of 1,000 points or 100 per cent. Actually, because of financial limitations and errors in planning, very few buildings rate over 800 points. Experience in rating numerous buildings in many communities indicates that plants rating above 700 points may be classified as very good buildings in terms of present practices. Plants scoring between 600 and 700 points are better than average, but usually lack some of the needed special facilities. Schools scoring between 400 and 500 points are below average, and need considerable modernization and

---

[3] Henry H. Linn and Felix J. McCormick, *School Plant Rating Form* (New York: Bureau of Publications, Teachers College, Columbia University, 1956).

rehabilitation. Buildings scoring less than 400 points are educationally obsolete and should usually be abandoned.

Computing capacity and utilization. The ultimate capacity of
any school building is the resultant of the quality of the educational
program. For example, a 20 classroom elementary school building
would have a capacity of 700 pupils based on an average class size
of 35 children. Improving the quality and cost of education by reducing the average class size to 25 pupils would reduce the operating
capacity of the building to 500 students. Each improvement in the
quality of education usually results in a reduction in the operating
capacity of the building. Lay citizens are frequently confused and
dismayed to discover that the old high school that formerly housed
2,000 students is now badly overcrowded with 1,500 pupils. They
fail to recognize that the necessary expansion of the library, guidance facilities, science laboratories, along with the installation of
small group seminar rooms, language laboratories, and other needed
improvements has drastically reduced the capacity of the building.
This continuing reduction of capacity represents an attempt to
modify obsolete structures to accommodate modern educational programs. Capacity, therefore, is a dynamic figure and one that should
continue to decline during the years ahead.

In comparing a number of school buildings within a school district, any computation of capacity should be stated as a comparative
capacity with the assumption of a relatively equal educational quality level. Equal, however, should not be equated with "sameness," as
each school's educational program should be designed to serve the
individual differences of each student and his community. Obviously, the program and building needs of a lower socioeconomic
area should be considerably different from the educational facilities
in a culturally favored area of the district. In fact, school buildings
serving the culturally disadvantaged typically require larger amounts
of space for their unique curriculum needs.

The following illustrations depict one common method of computing comparative capacities for a typical self-contained elementary
school and a departmentalized secondary school.

The elementary school described below has a desired capacity of
535 pupils. This capacity figure was derived by allocating 25 pupils
to each regular classroom, 20 pupils to each half-day kindergarten
session and 10 pupils to each class in special education and each
class for the visually handicapped. The overcrowded capacity was

ELEMENTARY SCHOOL CAPACITY

Number	Space	Desired Capacity	Overcrowded Capacity
17	Regular Classrooms	425	510
2	Kindergartens	80	100
2	Classrooms for Special Education	20	30
1	Classroom for the Visually Handicapped	10	15
1	Remedial Reading Center		
1	Library		
1	Special-Use Room		
1	Administrative Suite		
1	Multi-purpose Playroom		
1	Teachers Lounge		
1	Conference Room		
1	Small Basement Room		
	Total	535	655

determined by increasing each classroom, kindergarten, and special-use classroom by five pupils. Obviously, any increase or decrease in the assumed pupil-teacher ratio would change the capacity of the school.

During September of the current year, this elementary school had a total enrollment of 566. This enrollment of 566 exceeds the desired capacity by 31 pupils but is 89 students less than the building's

SECONDARY SCHOOL CAPACITY

Number	Space	Capacity Desired	Capacity Over-Crowded	Total Capacity Desired	Total Capacity Over-Crowded
2	Classrooms (regular)	25	30	50	60
36	Classrooms (small)	20	25	720	900
3	Biology Laboratories	24	28	72	84
2	Physics Laboratories	24	28	48	56
2	Chemistry Laboratories	24	28	48	56
1	Drafting Room	25	30	25	30
1	General Shop	24	28	24	28
2	Homemaking rooms	20	24	40	48
2	Typing Rooms	30	35	60	70
2	Art Rooms	24	28	48	56
1	Music Room	40	60	40	60
1	Boys' Gymnasium	35	45	35	45
1	Girls' Gymnasium	35	45	35	45
1	Auxiliary Gymnasium	15	20	15	20
1	Study Hall	60	90	60	90
	Total Gross Capacity			1,320	1,648
	Room Scheduling Factor			85%	85%
	Comparative Capacity			1,122	1,401

overcrowded capacity. Estimate of future enrollment shows a decline in estimated enrollment to 493 pupils five years later. This building has sufficient capacity to accommodate its present and future student body without the addition of new classrooms. In the future it may relieve a nearby overcrowded school by the use of minor adjustments in school attendance boundaries.

The senior high school illustrated above has a desired capacity of 1,122 students and an overcrowded capacity of 1,401 pupils. During the current school year the school had an actual enrollment of 1,798 students, or 397 students in excess of the building's overcrowded capacity. Estimates of future enrollments indicate an increase in enrollments to approximately 2,000 students. Obviously, this building will need a major addition or a major change in its school attendance boundary.

Summarizing the school building data. A careful study of the existing school buildings is one important part of a total school plant study. It usually includes development of corrected "single line" floor plans for each building, plot plans of each site, along with illustrative photographs of the school building, site, and surrounding neighborhood. Comparative capacities are computed for each school building and are analyzed in relationship to existing and future enrollments. The educational adequacy of each building is determined by the use of existing school building rating forms. Frequently the study includes the development of a list of needed improvements to each school. This list may be developed by utilizing a standardized checklist and by working with the building principal and his head custodian.

The data gathered in this portion of the total study is of considerable value to the survey team in formulating final recommendations. A summary table is frequently added to the final page of the school plant chapter to aid the survey team in their deliberations. The table provided on page 29 illustrates one method of summarizing the basic data:

From School Program to School Plant

Determining local school building needs should not be confused with the continuous and crucially important process of curriculum study and improvement. The school plant planner, however, must rely extensively on the curriculum specialist for the planning of

TABLE 6

SCHOOL PLANT SUMMARY

Name of School	Grades Housed	Educational Adequacy	No. of Needed Improvements	Comparative Capacity	Estimated Enrollment
Clay	K–6	76%	21	570	620
Holmes	K–6	84%	8	650	590
Seward	K–8	41%	64	310	215
Kenny	K–6	66%	28	710	905
Page	K–9	36%	65	370	405
Sanford	7–9	69%	27	790	870
Ramsay	7–9	51%	53	580	605
Central	10–12	63%	24	1140	1300

new school buildings and for assistance in developing decisions concerning the modernization or abandonment of existing structures.

Answers must be provided by the curriculum specialist to the following basic questions:

1. What is the existing and desired vertical school organization? (K–6–3–3, K–8–4–2, etc.)
2. What amount and kinds of spaces are needed to effectively carry out the existing and desired educational programs in each of the schools?
3. What is the recommended ideal size and acceptable range in size for the elementary and secondary schools?
4. What special services need to be provided in each of the schools?
5. What is the desirable range in class size for the various grade levels and special programs?
6. How will the school site be used?
7. How will the school serve its neighborhood service area?

The answers to the above questions should provide the survey team with partial criteria for evaluating each school building. These criteria, when combined with other factors such as safety, health, location, capacity, and structural characteristics, provide the basis for a careful evaluation of the educational facilities.

School programs are directly and sometimes adversely affected by the educational facilities in which they are housed. Educators endorse the idea that school buildings must be designed in such a manner that the facilities enhance the educational programs needed to serve the children of the district. Thus, good school buildings reflect current school programs and are flexible enough to be changed easily to meet future educational needs. In practice, a poorly planned building presents a major obstacle to effective daily teaching; it may also impede desirable changes in the curriculum.

It is important that any study of long-term school building needs include an examination of current educational programs and the evaluation of each school building in terms of the information gathered. It is also necessary that the survey team describe emerging trends in educational programs and appraise the implications of these trends with respect to existing and future school buildings. Actually, the program of the modern elementary, junior, and senior high school includes so much more than the traditional instruction of young people that it is necessary to be concerned with more than the formal school program—for example, community use of the school by adult groups must be included in the building evaluation.

Developing school building recommendations. It is suggested that a study of future school building needs may be logically divided into five sections or chapters. These sections are: (1) the School-Community, (2) School Enrollments, (3) Educational Facilities, (4) Educational Programs, and (5) Recommended School Building Program. Previous portions of this chapter have detailed the materials to be included in the four basic sections of the report. The major task remaining for the survey team is to develop final recommendations derived from the data previously compiled and analyzed.

Most surveys recognize the need to develop both long- and short-term recommendations. It is desirable to develop long-term recommendations, envisioning an ideal school plant some years hence, prior to outlining immediate needs. Unfortunately, some studies do not follow this procedure. A long-term plan is necessary and of considerable value in evaluating each short-term or immediate decision.

The recommended long-term plan. The planning principles formulated in the preceding section of this chapter are the foundation stones upon which to construct a long-term plan for the school building needs of the district. This section of the report should describe in broad outline the place of each school unit in the long-term plan. It should suggest the need for new buildings, new sites, additional facilities, additional acreage, modernization, rehabilitation, relocation, change in use, new programs, abandonment, and razing. It should project an image of the needed educational facilities for several decades into the future.

The recommended long-term plan proposes an ideal for the citizens of the school district to study and review. Future planning decisions should be considered in relationship to the long-term plan. It would be unwise, for example, to expend large sums of money on a major modernization of an obsolete school building that will not be continued as a part of a long-term plan. Future unforeseen actions by public bodies and individuals may necessitate modifications of this long-term plan. The changing of the proposed route of a future freeway is one example. The development and communication of this long-term plan should assist in the prevention of undesirable changes in total city and metropolitan planning.

Recommended first steps. The recommended first steps should represent the most urgent school building needs in the district. The cost of implementing all of the school district needs will usually exceed the legal debt limit placed upon the district by the state constitution or legislature. For this reason the survey team is forced to develop a list of priorities and to include only high priority projects in the recommended first steps. The "first steps" are just that; they will not solve all the new school building needs of the district, nor will they complete the necessary upgrading of each school building receiving attention. Additional steps will be needed at a future date to bring each school unit to the level of excellence desired by the citizens of the school district.

The recommended first steps are usually subdivided into categories such as:

    A. The Senior High Schools
    B. The Junior High Schools
    C. The Elementary Schools
    D. Special Education Facilities
    E. Construction Contingency
    F. Site Expansion

Each project recommended needs to be developed in sufficient detail to insure a clear understanding of the recommendation and its cost implications. However, the survey team should avoid detailed educational planning of a building or the attempt to develop elaborate and complicated cost estimates. This educational and architectural planning should follow the acceptance of the recommendations by the board of education and the provision of needed financial support.

The following example illustrates a suggested method of outlining a typical recommendation.

North Senior High School	*Estimated Costs*[4]
A. Site Acquisition	$ 300,000
B. First Addition	$ 500,000
1. Gym, Lockers, and Showers	
2. Music Suite	
C. Modernization and Rehabilitation	$ 400,000
1. Industrial Arts (Furniture and Equipment)	
2. Art Rooms (Furniture and Equipment)	
3. Home Economics (Furniture and Equipment)	
4. Science Rooms (Furniture and Equipment)	
5. Lockers	
D. Limited Maintenance and Repair in Old Building	$ 175,000
E. Upgraded Communication System	$ 15,000
F. Minor Improvements	$ 100,000
1. Classrooms	
2. Instructional Materials Center	
3. Educational and Custodial Storage	
Total	$1,490,000

As soon as any study is printed, it begins to become obsolete. Decisions made by public and private groups will affect its obsolescence more and more rapidly as the years go by. The wise and prudent planner continuously reviews his findings, revises or modifies his recommendations where necessary, and proposes new solutions in the light of additional information. It is incumbent upon the local school district that they require such periodic reviews, revisions, and new proposals.

---

[4] Includes site acquisition, construction contracts, furniture and equipment, site development, and architectural fees.

CHAPTER III

Planning a School Building

The previous chapter drew a distinction between planning *for* school buildings and the planning *of* a school building. It was suggested that planning for school buildings is the initial step in planning and is concerned with the development of a recommended long-term school building program. Planning of school buildings involves developing the educational and architectural plans leading to the actual construction of a new educational facility. It may be described as translating the desired educational program into a physical structure. One prominent educator has succinctly stated the case for clear, concise, and complete educational specifications as follows:

> Many kinds of facilities can be of assistance in implementing quality teaching and quality learning. The most important of these is the school building and its equipment. Our goal is to provide more than classroom space; it is to provide the kind of space which will be a positive force in improving educational opportunities. Our objective is to provide buildings that in themselves are of educational value as tools . . . The architect needs much more than the obvious information such as the size and location of the site, the budget appropriation, and the number of children for whom he is to provide rooms. It is also necessary that the architect know the kind of learning experiences in which they will engage.[1]

The Planning Team

The planning team should include all individuals who will be involved in the development and interpretation of the educational specifications used to guide the architect in his planning. It is suggested that the following participate in the planning: (1) the board of education, (2) the superintendent of schools and his administrative staff, (3) a building principal, (4) selected teachers, (5)

---

[1] Benjamin C. Willis, *We Build, A Progress Report.* Annual Report of the Chicago Board of Education (Chicago, Illinois: Board of Education, 1958), pp. 4–7.

members of the student government, (6) custodians, (7) representative citizens, (8) curriculum specialists, (9) educational consultants specializing in the planning of educational facilities, and (10) the architect selected to design the building.

Each member of the planning team has a different role and changing responsibilities as the planning progresses. Each individual should clearly understand his advisory relationship to the board of education and should operate within his sphere of technical competence. The superintendent of schools, or his designated representative, should serve as the chief executive officer or chairman in the development of the recommended educational specifications. The board of education has the legal responsibility for final determination of what kind of building should be constructed. This legal responsibility may be accomplished by the review, revision, and adoption of the recommended educational specifications, along with approval or rejection of building plans submitted by the architect. Acceptance or rejection of actual construction bids is another major responsibility of the school board.

Developing Educational Specifications

A school building is more than a physical structure providing housing, light, heat, and shelter from the elements. It is one expression of the community's commitment to education. It reflects a host of values concerning the worth and dignity of the individual. The building may be aesthetically exciting or ugly with no significant difference in cost. It may encourage educational change or make such change virtually impossible to attain. The primary function of a school building is to assist in the attainment of a desired educational program for a specified group of individuals. Educational specifications are designed to guide the architect in planning the kind of building desired by the educational planners.

Educational specifications have ranged from a single page listing the number of students to be housed and the building budget, to a comprehensive discussion of the activities to be conducted in each space, the relationships between spaces, and the characteristics of the educational program. Complete and carefully developed specifications make it more likely that the architect will be able to design a school building that will meet the comprehensive educational needs

of the school-community. If sufficient time is budgeted for educational planning, then the planning of a school building may achieve
the additional function of serving as a "triggering" device for major
curriculum improvements.

One set of comprehensive educational specifications for elementary schools contains the following major components:

1. Introduction
2. The Objectives and Goals of Elementary Education
3. General Principles of Design
4. Program of Requirements
5. Kindergarten Rooms
6. Primary Classrooms
7. Classrooms for the Intermediate Grades
8. Instructional Materials Center
9. Administrative Center
10. Adjustment Room
11. Health Room
12. Multi-Purpose Room
13. Elementary Playroom
14. Educational Storage Spaces
15. Teachers' Rooms
16. Toilet Rooms
17. Custodial Areas and Mechanical Area
18. Circulation Spaces
19. Recommended Illumination Criteria
20. Concerning Beauty in Building[2]

One of the most extensive educational specifications ever developed for secondary schools was prepared by the Detroit Public
Schools for their current school building program. They were as-
sisted by a grant from the Ford Foundation. A partial outline of
their specifications illustrate the comprehensiveness of their educational planning guide:

I. The Eastern High School Area
II. The People: Characteristics and Aspirations
III. Community Services
IV. The Educational Program
   A. We Believe
   B. Educational Background and Aspirations of the Community
   C. Prospective Enrollment

---

2 John J. McNicholas, Jr. and Donald J. Leu, *Developing Elementary School
Educational Specifications* (East Lansing, Michigan: College of Education, Michigan State University, 1961), p. iii.

    D. Offerings
          Language Arts
          Fine Arts
          Living Arts
          Science and Industrial Arts
    E. Organization of the Educational Program
    F. Organization of Counseling Programs and Services
    G. Personnel
    H. Evaluation
  V. Spaces Which Need to be Provided
    A. Eastern High School
    B. The Family Center
    C. Organization of Rooms and Spaces
 VI. Performance Specifications for Rooms and Spaces
    A. Academic House
    B. Resource and Materials Center
    C. Manipulative Skills Area
    D. Health and Physical Education Area
    E. Performing Arts
    F. Administrative Services
    G. Service Areas
    H. The Family Center[3]

These specifications were cooperatively developed by a planning team composed of school building planning specialists, subject-area specialists, teachers, representatives from related governmental agencies (City Plan Commission, Department of Parks and Recreation, Commission on Children and Youth, etc.), citizens, school principals, university consultants, and other specialists. One year was allowed for the educational planning. This creative and comprehensive educational planning has returned rich educational dividends to the citizens of Detroit. The resultant educational facilities represent a major improvement in the educational adequacy of the new school facilities. Perhaps more important than the changing physical structures is the fact that the planning of the new schools has served as a stimulus for curriculum study and improvement.

The educational program. The desired educational program should provide the basic foundation for planning educational facilities. In the final analysis the value of a new school building cannot be accurately measured in dollars and cents; the new school must be evaluated in terms of its ability to efficiently and effectively carry

---

[3] *Recommendations for New Eastern High School and Family Center* (Detroit, Michigan: Board of Education, January, 1963), pp. xvii–xxiii.

out a specified educational program. Unfortunately, many educational specifications either omit a careful description of the educational program or state the program objectives in such vague terms that they are of little assistance to the architect in reaching his design solutions. The development of the general goals and objectives of education should precede a description of the functions of individual spaces. Imbalance of facilities, omission of needed spaces, or inclusion of low priority spaces frequently result when each subject-area group plans independently of the over-all curriculum guide. A recommended procedure in developing educational specifications is to move from the general to the specific and from long-term goals to immediate objectives.

An excellent example of an educational program statement is provided by the Detroit Public Schools. Portions of it read as follows:

> We Believe: A Statement of Convictions About Education.
> . . . Today's students need an increased knowledge of languages, both their own and others, world geography, political organizations of other countries as well as their own, physical and biological sciences, and the nature of the productive organization. A new high school in the heart of the city must provide understanding of the urban society of which it is a part. It must change as the urban society changes. We believe that the fullest use should be made of all instructional materials, resources, and equipment which will enrich the experience of students who come to the school from a limited background . . . We believe that the new Eastern High School should build a program that meets the needs of students over the full range of ability, both the gifted and those with special needs. . . .
> We believe that it is essential to organize the counseling program so that each student can be helped to an understanding of his individual needs and abilities without being classified as to general ability or a prescribed curriculum.
> We believe that it is important for each student in the school to have some adult or adults whom he comes to know well and continuously through his high school years. . . .
> We believe that there are essential democratic values in having students of all ability groups and viewpoints participating in basic courses together. . . .[4]

These strong statements on educational philosophy and objectives give clear direction to the architect in his planning. The inherent worth and dignity of each individual is made clear. Individual dif-

---

[4] *Ibid.*, pp. 43–44.

ferences are recognized and physical facilities must provide for them. Statements indicating the dynamic character of the school and community make it obvious that the building must permit frequent curriculum changes. The program objectives indicate that a considerable portion of the building must be committed to counseling purposes, and library-like spaces. Decentralization of large groups into smaller and more personalized groupings is indicated. Actually, a "house-plan" or clusters of "little-schools" evolved from the program statements. Perhaps the greatest contribution of the program objectives was a radical departure from the typical school design of many metropolitan schools. These older schools feature a prison-like atmosphere with row after row of unrelated cell-blocks. It would be difficult indeed to interpret Detroit's program specifications into a typical school of the past.

Program of requirements. Educational specifications should include a statement of the spaces to be provided in the school building. This program of requirements is actually a summary of the detailed planning for each individual space. Frequently this space analysis may be reviewed by the architect in order to determine the estimated cost of providing the required spaces. If the building budget has been determined prior to the completion of the educational specifications, this document may then serve as a "checkpoint" to determine whether or not the desired building may be provided within the budgeted monies. The following outline is suggested for developing the program requirements for an elementary school:

   I. Planning Committee (include name and title of chairman)
  II. Site Information (size and location)
 III. Construction Budget
 IV. Grades to be Housed
  V. Capacity of School (include method of computing capacity)
 VI. Space Requirements (number and size)
    A. Kindergartens
    B. Primary Classrooms
    C. Intermediate Classrooms
    D. Instructional Materials Center
    E. Administrative Spaces
    F. Special Rooms
    G. Educational Storage Space
    H. Teachers' Rooms
    I. Custodial Areas

J. Toilet Rooms
K. Circulation Spaces
L. Outdoor educational and recreational spaces
VII. Planning Time Schedule

The above outline may be easily adapted to serve a junior or senior high school. When the architect is included as a member of the original planning team, it then becomes possible to utilize his specialized skills in developing a more detailed program of requirements. The architect, for example, working as a member of the planning team, may develop estimates of squarefootage required to serve each of the desired spaces. These estimates are based on the information provided him by the educational planners. The program requirements for a junior college (Table 7) illustrate this method:

TABLE 7

SUMMARY OF BUILDING REQUIREMENTS *

	Gross Area (square feet)	Gross Expansion Allowance (square feet)
A. Administration	9,110	1,667
B. Library	25,595	4,175
C. Health, Physical Education, Recreation	45,710	3,340
D. Humanities Division	44,025	10,938
E. Science and Mathematics Division	36,120	22,300
F. Social Science Division	13,940	2,000
G. Business Education Division	9,820	4,000
H. Engineering and Technology Division	11,090	13,000
I. Student Union	18,900	5,678
J. Maintenance and Operations Division	11,231	–0–
Total	225,541	67,098

* Source: *Program of Preliminary Planning Requirements, Cabrillo College* (Palo Alto, California: Ernst J. Kump and Masten, Hurd and Gwathmey, Architects Associated, 1962).

It should be noted that the program requirements represent a summary of the detailed analysis of each space. Each building and space was carefully studied by the planning team in terms of its capacity, function, and relationship to the other components of the total school plant. The library, for example, provided one portion of the summary program of requirements. The development of the spaces required for the library is illustrated in Table 8.

TABLE 8

LIBRARY BUILDING *

	Initial Stage		Expansion Allowance	
	No.	Area	No.	Area
Gross Allowance		25,595		
Allowance for Circulation		5,380		
Sub-total: Area Excluding Circulation		20,215		
Allowance for General Service and Structure		4,040		
Net Usable Area		16,175		
Library Services				
1. Reading Rooms	2	4,500	1	2,500
2. Reference Room	1	2,500		
3. Book Stacks (10 study cubicles)	1	4,500		
4. Office: Librarian	1	300		
5. Office: Secretary	1	125		
6. Conference Room	1	300		
7. Work Room	1	900		
8. Typing Room, Group Study	7	1,100		
9. Faculty Reading Room, Kitchenette	1	600		
Audiovisual Section				
1. Office, files, film and record stacks	1	450		
2. Listening Room and Control Room	1	700		
3. Production, Maintenance, and Storage	1	300		
		16,175		

* Source: *Program of Preliminary Planning Requirements, Cabrillo College* (Palo Alto, California: Ernst J. Kump and Masten, Hurd and Gwathmey, Architects Associated, 1962).

All too frequently the planning team is not given sufficient time or human resources to do the quality of planning illustrated above. When this is true, the planners should realize that a detailed space analysis must be provided by the architect at a later date. They should develop their program of requirements in sufficient detail and correct form so that the architect may complete this facet of his task in an efficient manner. Many an architect has been criticized for his building when the basic fault lies in the low quality of educational planning preceding his work.

Room specifications. Room specifications are developed to aid the architect in designing each educational space. They express, in nontechnical terms, the physical "envelope" surrounding the students and their teacher. These specifications should not restrict the architect in his search for new and better materials or attempt to freeze new school design to past history. Educators should not attempt to play architect by presenting the school's architect with a set of clumsily drawn floor plans. The frequent practice of educators posing as amateur architects is sometimes humorous—but more often tragic. The purple-colored classroom and gymnasium-sized toilet room are classic examples of educators moving out of their sphere of technical competence. Not so obvious are the thousands of poor planning decisions resulting from room specifications which prohibit creative architectural planning.

Room specifications should clearly describe the following components of an educational space:

1. Activities engaged in by pupils and teacher.
2. Location of unit in relation to other spaces.
3. Equipment and storage requirements.
4. Special facilities or considerations unique to the space.

The following specifications for a kindergarten room provide an example of the needed description of activities:

Kindergarten Room—Activities

1. *Activity program.* There is a need for adequate space to provide varied project areas. For example, paint easels, work bench, and table are needed in addition to a number of other tables for coloring, pasting, and working with clay.
2. *Dramatic play activities.* Space is needed for a playhouse and for block building.
3. *Rhythmic activities.* Floor space is required for large muscle activities such as skipping and galloping. Children customarily sit in a large circle for this part of their program, using the space in the middle for their rhythmic interpretations. A piano is used with these activities.
4. *Use of floor.* Children often sit, play, or lie on the floor. Floors must be warm.
5. *Audiovisual aids.* An important part of the kindergarten program is the use of audiovisual aids, e.g., film projectors, filmstrips, phonographs, and television.
6. *Material preparation.* The teacher needs work space and sink for washing paint jars, mixing paints, and other jobs connected with the preparation of materials.[5]

The above description of activities should provide the architect with an understanding of the function of the room and how the

---

[5] McNicholas, *Elementary Educational Specifications, op. cit.,* pp. 21–22.

room will be used by the children and their teacher. His preliminary design solution may then be evaluated and revised in accordance with the room specifications.

The location of a room with respect to other facilities is also important information for the architect. Proper space relationships are a key factor in making a building effective. An outstanding library, for example, is of limited value if it is inaccessible to the group using it. The careful interrelationship of all the building's spaces and outside areas is one of the most difficult design problems facing the architect. Simple circle diagrams illustrating proposed space relationships is a most effective way of reaching a final solution.

Movable furniture and equipment is usually not provided in the construction cost of a building. The architect, therefore, is not paid a fee for providing this equipment. He should, however, be provided with a complete listing of all the furniture and equipment being planned for each space. His plans must "design in" all the furniture and equipment provided in the school. It is interesting to note that recent years have witnessed a tremendous increase in the amount and complexity of school equipment. Proper storage of this equipment is also of major importance.

General principles of design.   Worth of a completed school building will be judged by a number of standards, many of which reflect the background and interests of the individuals making the evaluation. Parents, teachers, and other citizens of the community generally agree that the primary purpose of the school building is to house the educational program. Beyond this point of general agreement, however, individuals decide in their own minds whether the building is good or bad by comparing the various facilities with some standard or value. For example, all parents are concerned with having their children housed in safe, comfortable buildings; many taxpayers consider economy of construction and operation as an important factor; other citizens are interested in the external appearance of the building; and educators will want to emphasize adequacy for housing the instructional program. Constructing a building which might rate high in terms of all of these criteria, as well as many others not mentioned, may be impossible in a practical situation because of limitations usually imposed by the amount of money available for school plant construction.

In spite of the wide range of criteria by which a building is judged, persons concerned with the important task of providing adequate housing for the school program need to develop a set of principles which will guide their activities and by which the completed building may be judged. Although the list of principles suggested below could be expanded, experience with school construction during recent years has convinced educators and architects that genuine consideration of these objectives will result in acceptable school buildings. The design principles usually agreed upon as being important are:

1. Safety
2. Health
3. Educational Adequacy
4. Economy
5. Flexibility
6. Expansibility
7. Aesthetics

Obviously, the architect cannot observe each of these principles in all of their implications. As was pointed out previously, economy may be a determining factor in the practical situation where flexibility might seem more important to those planning the school building. Because of the importance of achieving a balance of many factors involved in providing the best school building possible, cooperative planning by teachers, pupils, custodial staff, administrators, and architects will bring a variety of skills, kinds of knowledge, and insights to bear upon each decision as it needs to be made.

A brief mention of each of the design principles will be made in the succeeding paragraphs in order that those concerned with planning may develop their thinking around certain common ideas.

The principle of safety is mentioned first since, in the minds of parents at least, the safety of their children transcends all other considerations. (It has been said that parents prefer an uneducated child to one who is injured or killed in an unsafe school building.) Although safety is of basic importance as a design principle, it should always be considered along with educational adequacy. A school which does not adequately serve the educational program may be entirely safe; however, the goal should always be a safe and educationally adequate structure.

Safety is the concern of parents, teachers, and the children themselves; building design embodying requirements of building codes properly interpreted by the architect and contractor can result in safe buildings. For example:

Basic materials of construction should be fire resistive and of sufficient strength to insure structural soundness.

Corridors and exits should be well arranged, strategically located, and of sufficient width to care for children in case of emergency. Exits should be clearly marked by an emergency lighting system.

Stairs should be designed to minimize slipping or tripping.

Exit doors should be provided with panic fixtures.

Doors should be secure against intruders.

Site planning should minimize hazards connected with service driveways and parking areas near buildings or play areas.

Sufficient illumination should be provided for every space in the building. Outside lighting to minimize vandalism must also be considered.

In general, those charged with providing adequate schools must make use of all available information and techniques in order to safeguard the lives of children.

The school building should provide space in which teachers and children can work together in surroundings which are conducive to physical, mental, and emotional health. Teachers find it difficult to establish acceptable health habits and skills in surroundings which themselves do not meet recognized standards of health and comfort.

Attention to such items as the following will help in providing a school building which meets the criterion of health.

Toilet and water supplies should be ample, with proper regard for the requirements of children and employees as well as those fixed by the building code.

The heating and ventilating system, automatically controlled, should supply adequate amounts of tempered fresh air to all instructional spaces.

Any other area of the building which is to be occupied by faculty or the public (such as administration, adjustment, and health rooms) should be adequately heated and ventilated.

A variety of pleasing colors, appropriate acoustical treatment, and comfortable seating will contribute materially to mental and emotional health of children and teachers.

A balanced visual environment should be provided by means of artificial and natural light of the proper amount and quality.

Building design should be such that the various rooms can be kept clean and in a good state of repair with a minimum of effort on the part of the maintenance and custodial staff.

As has been mentioned previously, there is general agreement upon the fact that the primary purpose of the school building is to house the educational program. Therefore, educational adequacy is an important principle of design and should be observed in constructing a school building. In fact, educational adequacy is of such importance that any thought of its subordination to other considerations must be carefully analyzed. Further evidence of its significance is borne out by a consideration of its meaning in terms of the learning process.

Educational adequacy suggests appropriate space in which children, guided by competent teachers, will live and learn together and grow as individuals, physically, mentally, and socially.

To grow physically, children need ample indoor and outdoor facilities suited to their varying ages and sizes. To grow mentally, children need to work and study in large, well-lighted, well-ventilated, attractively decorated classrooms and libraries with a variety of equipment and instructional materials suited to their maturity levels. To grow socially, to develop wholesome personalities and learn to live democratically, children need large spaces for group activities, small spaces where noisy work can go on without disturbing others, and appropriate facilities for developing creative expression.

Though indirectly affecting the growth of children, but just as critical, are the needs of school staff members. Conference rooms for meetings with parents and other staff members, storage space for instructional materials, filing facilities for records and reference materials, space for preparation of materials, and rooms for relaxing at meals and at appropriate moments during the school day all contribute to staff efficiency and, subsequently, to a better instructional program.

Still another contribution which a well-planned school building can make, although not directly connected with the instructional program for children, is the provision for community use of the building. With decreased working hours and increased use of labor saving machinery, the general population enjoys unprecedented hours of leisure time. The community can, therefore, utilize the school facilities to an extent greater than ever before for evening educational, recreational, and cultural activities. The planning of the building should reflect this development in American life and encourage the community use of the school plant by design which facilitates these activities, although always protecting its primary use for education.

Consideration of the preceding requirements for an adequate school building makes clear the fact that those people who plan and construct a school building can contribute significantly to the instructional program by providing the necessary facilities.

Like some of the other criteria, economy has many connotations. The writer believes that true economy is the maximum educational return for each dollar spent. To some people economy means buying everything at the lowest price without regard for the purpose to be served. Applying the principle to the latter definition will undoubtedly result in the sacrifice of quality in important phases of the program. On the other hand, it is common knowledge that high price and high quality are not synonymous. The problem of educators and architects in planning school buildings, therefore, is to provide facilities of the proper quality and quantity for the specific job to be done. To accomplish this, materials must be judged for durability, function, appearance, and cost. Design should eliminate as much waste space as possible, since on the basis of economy, the worth of a school building is judged by the amount of instructional space provided for the money spent. Flexibility and expansibility, therefore, are important determiners of economy.

Omission of needed space or facilities which curtails the educational program or reduces staff efficiency is not real economy. Since the largest portion of the educational budget goes for instruction (teachers' salaries and supplies), the annual loss in staff efficiency can more than outweigh money saved in skimping on needed facilities.

The architect should consider the following items in planning a building for economy.

Before deciding upon single or multi-story construction, all factors such as building size, site size and topography, structural materials, and educational philosophy must be carefully considered.

Simple building layouts usually serve the educational program better than more complicated ones.

Use of standard equipment is encouraged. It should be moveable. Built-in units should be avoided wherever possible, but void spaces in walls can be utilized for built-in storage facilities.

A minimum of ornamentation is necessary.

Ease of maintenance and operation is an important consideration. Easy access should be provided for service lines which may require maintenance.

Overdesign of structural, heating, ventilating, plumbing, and electrical systems results in increased costs.

Competent supervision of the construction work is essential.

In the final analysis, teachers, citizens, and children must feel that the school building adequately serves their varied needs and, at the same time, has not cost an unreasonable amount of money for construction.

Since education is a dynamic force, changes in its character are continually taking place. Thus, methods and materials which today are integral parts of the educational program may become obsolete as scientific research develops new and better ways of teaching children. Changing educational objectives and methods may, therefore, dictate modifications in the original design of the building. If the school is constructed with the principle of flexibility in mind, it may be changed economically and efficiently.

Walls and partitions which may be moved at a later time should not contain heating, ventilating, plumbing, or main electrical lines which will be difficult to relocate. A minimum of built-in cupboards or other equipment should be placed in these walls.

Structural design of floor slabs as well as fenestration should permit the location of partitions at any convenient point.

Future expansion of the school plant may become necessary because of anticipated increases in school enrollments (considered in the planning of the original building), but unforeseen contingencies, being less easily defined, may be overlooked. Obviously, if the type of facilities which may be needed later can be outlined, even vaguely, somewhat more specific provision can be made in the initial construction.

Certain design features incorporated in the school building will facilitate future expansion.

Plumbing, electrical, and heating lines should be extended to points which will require these services at a later time.

Stairs should be placed at corridor sides rather than in ends to make future building expansion easier.

Classrooms should not be built across ends of building wings because this would prevent easy expansion.

Sufficient extra capacity should be allowed in electrical panels and conduits and plumbing and heating lines to meet reasonable future needs.

Boiler room space should be sufficient for additional boiler installation if an addition is needed at some future date.

Modern school buildings with their emphasis upon function should also add architectural beauty to a community. Current thinking concerning the appearance of buildings of all types places emphasis upon simplicity of form and line and utility. The school building is no longer conceived as a monument. The varieties of shape and mass required by the difference in educational needs provide the architect with many opportunities to design an interesting and beautiful school building. Rooms, furniture, and equipment should be scaled for children. A generous use of color (vivid primary ones should be adopted), to make the classroom a friendly, workable place. Honest, functional architecture can produce a building which is attractive in appearance to both adults and children. Useless pillars, towers, cupolas, and other ornamentation do not necessarily provide an appropriate atmosphere for a school building.

Citizens in the community who live near the school building will want its design to be consistent with, but not limited by, prevailing architecture of other structures in the immediate vicinity. Thus, the criterion of aesthetics challenge the artistic ability of the architect as he synthesizes the educational elements of the school building and site into a functional unit.

Although strict observance of the foregoing design principles will not alone insure a completely acceptable school building, they will serve as an important basis for critically evaluating many of the considerations on which specific decisions will be made during the course of planning and construction.

Selecting the School Architect

The school architect should be employed in the early stages of the school building program. His selection is the responsibility of the local board of education. The board's decision on the selection of an architectural firm is the key to a successful building program. The superintendent of schools should serve as the chief executive officer in securing information concerning available architectural firms and in providing information to those firms whose employment is being considered. Frequently the board of education will request the superintendent of schools to recommend an architectural firm for their selection or to narrow the field of candidates to a few firms prior to formal interview and selection.

The selection process may be simplified by utilizing the "Standard Form of Questionnaire for Selection of Architects for School Building Project."[6] This questionnaire was cooperatively developed and adopted by the American Institute of Architects and the National Council on Schoolhouse Construction. The form may be sent to local or national architectural firms to inform them of the proposed building project and it may guide the local district in the process of screening, interviewing, and selection of an architectural firm.

Qualifications of the architect. It is difficult for a lay board of education to accurately determine the qualifications of an architectural firm. A careful investigation of the firm is one method of evaluation. Adequate time should be provided for a complete review of the firm's qualifications to provide the quantity and quality of services desired. Visits to buildings recently completed by the architectural firm are another way of becoming better acquainted with the architect's work. Discussions between school administrators and board members previously involved with the architect will provide additional insight into the architect's ability to work closely and harmoniously with the total planning team.

---

6 Copies of this form are available from local chapters of the American Institute of Architects or from the Executive Secretary of the National Council on Schoolhouse Construction, College of Education, Michigan State University, East Lansing, Michigan.

The following evaluative criteria should be valuable in the selection process:

1. The architect should be legally qualified to practice in the state and should be in good standing in his profession. He must be a man of unquestioned professional character and integrity, and must possess high ethical standards.
2. The architect should have had previous successful experience in designing buildings which demonstrate his competence in architectural work. The buildings previously designed by the architect should also reflect a careful study of the peculiar needs of each client.
3. The architect should possess the vision and imagination to translate the educational aims and program specified by the educator into functional buildings. There should be an avoidance of stereotypes. The architect should not possess set, preconceived ideas which are hard to change. He must be able and willing to mold design to fit needs.
4. The architect must have a record of working cooperatively and harmoniously with his clients, educational advisors, and contractors.
5. The architect must have an adequate staff of trained personnel to carry out the building program without undue delay. The architect should either have qualified engineering services available in his own organization or should specify qualified engineering specialists who will work with him.
6. The architect should keep abreast of recent research and study concerning materials and mechanical equipment used in school buildings.
7. The architect should show such economy in the use of space and materials as is consistent with educational needs.
8. The architect should be competent in the field of site planning and the utilization of space for educational and recreational purposes.
9. The architect must give adequate supervision to his buildings. This is a very important part of the architect's services.
10. The architect should be informed concerning state and municipal building regulations and codes and must show care in complying with them.
11. The architect must demonstrate sound business judgment, proper business procedures, and good record keeping on the job.[7]

Architectural services. Many school districts do not make efficient or complete use of the architect's services. Frequently they are

---

[7] *Planning Together for Better School Buildings.* Brochure of the Michigan Department of Public Instruction (Lansing, Michigan: The Department, 1956), p. 26.

not aware of the basic services the architect has to offer and which services they are entitled to as a part of his contract fee. A contract agreement should be completed with the architect prior to any professional services being requested by the board of education or provided by the architectural firm. The American Institute of Architects has developed standard forms for this purpose. Usually this standard contract form may be adapted to meet local conditions.

Boards of education should avoid contracting with those few firms who violate the ethics of their profession by promising something for nothing in order to secure the contract. For example, the offer to provide free preliminary plans, or to develop detailed cost estimates, or promising to build the school cheaper than any other firm illustrates a clear violation of professional ethics. The acceptance of such offers may result in a commitment to an incompetent firm which precludes careful and creative planning.

The services of the school architect may be categorized into five important phases: (1) preparing preliminary plans and sketches, (2) preparing the working drawings and bid specifications, (3) assisting the board of education in the construction bidding, (4) assisting in the preparation of contract documents, and (5) supervision of construction.

Preliminary plans and specifications are developed by the architect as recommended design solutions to the educational specifications previously approved by the board of education. It is advantageous to have the architect work closely with the planning team in the development and interpretation of the educational specifications. This type of cooperative planning necessitates the early selection and employment of the architectural firm. Several months of planning time should be budgeted for the careful development, review, and revision of preliminary sketches, space relationship studies, and preliminary plans. The final preliminary sketches approved by the board of education should include floor plans, elevations and sections, site plans, and the drafting of brief outline specifications upon which tentative cost estimates can be prepared.

The development of working drawings and specifications follow the approval of preliminary sketches. These drawings and specifications describe the architectural, structural, mechanical (plumbing, heating, ventilating, and air-conditioning), and electrical components of the building in such detail as to enable the competing contractors to prepare their bid estimates and to construct the building as designed by the architect. Detailed layouts (illustrating the details of each wall, floor, and ceiling) should be included. These detailed layouts should be reviewed with the various subject-area specialists prior to approval by the board. All too frequently a beautiful building is nonfunctional because science specialists, librarians, physical education instructors, or other competent specialists were not given the opportunity to eliminate the "bugs" in the architect's plans.

Competent architects can save their clients a considerable amount of money by providing assistance concerning procedures to be followed in soliciting bids. This guidance is usually done in cooperation with the school board's attorney. These services normally include:

1. Preparing advertisement for bids.
2. Suggesting the most advantageous period of the year for soliciting construction bids.
3. Distributing a sufficient number of sets of plans and specifications during the bidding period.
4. Clarifying plans and specifications during the bidding period.
5. Assisting in the opening of bids.
6. Tabulating and analyzing bids after opening.
7. Checking performance and financial records of the low bidders.
8. Making recommendations to the board of education regarding the awarding of contracts.

Contract documents should be properly prepared and filed by the board of education, the architect, and the contractor. These documents should include the working drawings and specifications, including any addendums or changes adopted during the bidding period. Correctly executed surety bond forms and certificates of required insurance, along with a contract form signed by the board and contractor, should be on file. Assistance in the careful executing of all required legal documents avoids many costly legal entanglements among the board of education, contractors, and the architect.

The supervision of construction is one area of considerable confusion and misunderstanding. Prior to engaging an architect, a complete agreement should be reached regarding the amount and type of supervision to be provided by the architect. Normally the architect, in carry out his supervision of construction, will endeavor to protect the owner against defects or omissions in the work of the various contractors. The architect will not, however, guarantee the performance of the construction contracts. Periodic architectural supervision should be distinguished from the continuous supervision provided by the employment of a "clerk-of-the-works."

Many boards of education, particularly on larger construction projects, deem it a wise investment to employ a full-time or part-time person who will oversee the building of the school. This practice decreases the possibility of being "short-changed by a contractor." There should be a clear understanding among the school board, the "clerk-of-the-works," architect, contractors, workmen, and school administrators regarding the authority and responsibility of the "clerk-of-the-works." Excellent working drawings and specifications have often been subverted by inadequate or incompetent supervision. Delays in construction time, legal entanglements, and financial losses may occur as the result of inadequate construction supervision.

Selecting the School Site

Prior to planning the school building, a site for the school must be selected and purchased. Many school districts select sites on the basis of too few facts; others take no action to acquire land until the damage of land development has been done. After the floodgates of new housing construction have been opened and previously undeveloped land has been covered with new homes, there is frequently no remaining acceptable land available for adequate or correctly located school sites.

Both the taxpayers and the school children pay for this lack of foresight. Ultimately, land must be purchased at an inflated price, to which must be added the expense of condemnation and building removal. The cost of constructing the building often mounts, owing to excessive charges for grading, drainage, installing service facilities, and the necessity of complicated and expensive footings. Sometimes there is the cost of transporting children as the result of a forced acceptance of a site located beyond a reasonable walking distance from their homes. These and other hidden costs are passed on to the taxpayer over the ensuing years.

The educational program of a school which is located on a small, inadequate site is of necessity seriously curtailed. This distressing situation commonly continues for 50 years or more during the building's usable life. School site selection must not be a policy of "too little and too late"; instead it must be taken out of the area of guesswork and political pressures and placed within the field of a comprehensive analysis of long-term school plant needs.

Four basic points should be considered in evaluating potential sites: size, topography, location, and cost. The following rating form has been developed to aid school districts in selecting their school sites.

It should be cautioned that any rating form cannot evaluate in sufficient detail all the information required in selecting a school site. Furthermore, the weighing of each individual item may differ among communities. For example, the standards of site size may of necessity vary between large city school districts and schools located in suburban communities. Nevertheless, the use of a rating form will insure that each of the major points is carefully considered.

Visual illustrations provide a valuable means for evaluating proposed school sites and for informing the citizens of the community as to the need for additional sites. There is little merit in wise site selection if the voters or local governing agency will not approve the site acquisition proposal. Maps provide the most effective type of illustration, while other tools such as charts, graphs, tables, slides, and overlays are also useful. Although there is no specific number of maps required to depict clearly the particular site problems of each community, the following kinds of maps form an adaptable basis:

1. Location of School Pupils (spot map)
2. Location of Existing and Proposed Dwelling Units (spot map)
3. Location of Existing and Proposed Major Traffic Arteries
4. Existing and Proposed Zoning Plan
5. Land-Use Map
6. Location of Existing and Proposed School Sites (with circles illustrating distances)
7. Plot Plan of Proposed School Sites (special features, adjoining streets, and service connections indicated)
8. Topographical Map of the Proposed Site

Preferably, school sites should be purchased far in advance of actual need. Ten years, five years, or even one year hence is often too late to acquire an adequate site at a reasonable cost. Too frequently school districts have been saddled for another half-century with unsuitable leftovers. Estimated future school enrollments, com-

TABLE 9

RATING FORM FOR THE SELECTION
OF SCHOOL SITES *

INSTRUCTIONS: Score items as follows: 5 = Very Superior, 4 = Superior, 3 = Average, 2 = Below Average, 1 = Poor, 0 = Very Poor. Multiply score "times" weight and enter result in total column.

BASIC CONSIDERATIONS	SCORE	WEIGHT	TOTAL	GRAND TOTAL	NOTES
I. *Size*				——	
A. Size	—— ×	60 =	——		
B. Expansibility	——	20	——		
II. *Topography*				——	
A. Elevation	——	10	——		
B. Drainage	——	10	——		
C. Soil	——	10	——		
D. Contour	——	10	——		
E. Shape	——	5	——		
F. Natural Features	——	3	——		
G. Attractiveness	——	2	——		
III. *Location*				——	
A. Central Location	——	5	——		
B. Type of Neighborhood	——	5	——		
C. Zoning	——	5	——		
D. Accessibility	——	5	——		
E. Traffic Arteries	——	3	——		
F. Water Lines	——	3	——		
G. Sewers	——	2	——		
H. Electricity	——	2	——		
I. Gas Lines	——	1	——		
J. Fire Protection	——	2	——		
K. Public Transportation	——	2	——		
L. Parks and Playgrounds	——	2	——		
M. Natural Hazards	——	1	——		
N. Noise	——	1	——		
O. Odors and Dust	——	1	——		
IV. *Cost*				——	
A. First Cost	——	10	——		
B. Site Development	——	5	——		
C. Building Removal	——	5	——		
D. Installation of Utilities	——	5	——		
E. Street Development	——	5	——		
		Grand Total	——		

* Source: Henry H. Linn, Felix J. McCormick, and Donald J. Leu, *Rating Form for the Selection of School Sites* (New York: Teachers College, Columbia University, 1954).

pared with the computed capacity of the existing school plant, can provide the basis for the early determination of school site needs. Careful selection of the school site will pay large educational and financial dividends during the years ahead.

Site size. The major reason for early obsolescence of many school buildings has been school sites which are too small in size and improperly located. The National Council on Schoolhouse Construction suggests the following size guidelines:

1. For elementary schools, it is suggested that there be provided a minimum site of 5 acres plus an additional acre for each 100 pupils of predicted ultimate maximum enrollment. Thus, the site of a minimum size for an elementary school of 200 pupils would be 12 acres.
2. For junior high schools, it is suggested that there be provided a minimum site of 20 acres plus an additional acre for each 100 pupils or projected ultimate maximum enrollment. Thus a site of minimum size for a junior high school of 500 pupils would be 25 acres.
3. For senior high schools, it is suggested that there be provided a minimum site of 30 acres plus an additional acre for each 100 pupils of projected ultimate maximum enrollment. Thus, the site of minimum size for a senior high school of 1,000 pupils would have a site of 40 acres.[8]

Obviously, the above suggested site sizes must be treated as a guide and not a standard. Favored school districts should exceed suggested minimum site sizes. Older congested cities will frequently have to compromise on the desirable site size and resort to compact design utilizing multi-story and below-ground spaces. Each school site has its own unique variations which must be analyzed before selecting the site.

[8] *Guide for Planning School Plants* (East Lansing, Michigan: National Council on Schoolhouse Construction, 1964), p. 27.

CHAPTER IV

School Building Modernization

School districts throughout the United States are faced with the continuous problem of modernizing, abandoning, or replacing their obsolescent school buildings. Frequently the decision is a complex one. Actually, all school buildings become partially obsolete prior to completion of initial construction. Obsolescence is a question of degree. Each succeeding year witnesses an increase in the degree of obsolescence. Obsolescence can be structural or educational, or the result of changing population centers. Most overaged school buildings, however, are structurally sound and educationally obsolete.

An analysis of the schools in one large city revealed buildings ranging in age from one to eighty-seven years. One hundred and twenty-six buildings were 40 years or older in age. This number represents approximately 45 per cent of the city's school buildings. The average age for these 126 buildings was approximately 53 years. A current 90 million dollar building program will result in replacing 19 of these older structures. When this major construction program is completed, 54 additional buildings will have attained the age of 40 years or older, or, expressed in another way, approximately 53.5 per cent of the total school buildings in the city will be in this age category. The net result of this large building program is a continued increase in the average age of the district's school buildings. These facts are typical of most of our major cities. Obviously, what to do with overaged and obsolete educational facilities is a major problem facing educational planners during the immediate years ahead.

School programs are directly and often adversely affected by the facilities in which they are housed. If the walls of a classroom, for example, define too little space for the attainment of desired educational objectives, the program must be curtailed. If these walls are of a "load-bearing" type, commonly found in older school buildings, their removal or relocation is virtually impossible. Thus the obsolete school building may seriously restrict the educational program.

It is a relatively simple matter for the lay public to determine the inability of a 1920 automobile to serve a modern society. Yet thousands of "Model T" classrooms are currently attempting to serve a "space age" curriculum for another five, ten, or twenty years. In addition to their educational limitations, these obsolete classrooms usually result in higher unit costs for maintenance and operation. For these reasons most school plant consultants regard 40 to 60 years as a maximum use span for educational facilities, even though the shell of the building might withstand the elements for 100 years or more.

Modernization, Replacement, or Abandonment

When the school building has reached a degree of obsolescence making it virtually impossible to carry on a modern program of education, the building must be abandoned, modernized, or replaced. Determining the degree of obsolescence, therefore, is a continuous problem facing educational planners. The following general criteria are suggested as an aid in determining the degree of obsolescence:

1. The school plant should provide a neighborhood or community center for people of all ages.
2. It should provide safe shelter for its occupants.
3. It should be economical in its costs of operation and maintenance.
4. It should expand, convert, and contract readily and economically as educational programs change.
5. It should foster, through its design of spaces, a variety of face-to-face human relations among its occupants.
6. It should provide a healthful and stimulating thermal, acoustical, and lighting environment keyed to the multiple activities of people.
7. It should facilitate changes in school organization by permitting varying separations among age groups, between noisy and quiet activities, and between the occupants' varying needs for social satisfaction and privacy.
8. It should bring service facilities within easy access of the people who require them.
9. It should merchandise the processes as well as the products of public education.
10. It should provide ample space for people actively engaged in a variety of educational experiences.
11. It should, above all, reflect in its form, scale, color, materials, and aesthetics a basic regard for the dignity and worth of the people who will use the building.

The above general criteria make it obvious that most older school buildings, resembling a series of unrelated "egg crates," fall far short of approaching acceptable educational standards.

Abandonment. Ideally, all overaged and obsolete school buildings should be abandoned for educational use or replaced with new functional school buildings. Unfortunately this solution is frequently fiscally impossible. Prior to investing large sums of money in the modernization or replacement of overaged school buildings, careful consideration should be given to the possibility of abandoning the school. Many older school buildings are located in the "core" area of the metropolitan complex. Tremendous changes have taken place in the schools' service area. Frequently the area has changed from residential to commercial or industrial. New or future freeways may remove large blocks of residential area. City or metropolitan plans for the future may further reduce the schools' long-term enrollment potential.

Careful study should precede any major investment of capital outlay expenditures in an old, obsolete, and poorly located educational facility. One basic question should be answered prior to modernizing or replacing an obsolete building: Is there a need for this type of school at this location for an extended period of time?

Substantial sums of money have been spent in the modernization of obsolete facilities which have continued to decline in school enrollment during future years. These unwise expenditures could have been avoided if long-term planning had preceded short-term or immediate decisions.

The best single method for determining a need for the continuation of an obsolete school is by the development of a long-term enrollment estimate for the school's service area. This enrollment estimate should be related to the changing population characteristics of the area. Zoning ordinances and the patterns of growth or decline of the residential area are most useful in arriving at long-term enrollment estimates.[1] Spot maps illustrating the number and location of preschool and school children are useful in determining the feasibility of the children being served by adjacent schools. Dwelling unit maps showing the location and type of old, new, and proposed dwelling units furnish additional valuable information to the planner.

---

[1] For a more detailed description of procedures for estimating school enrollments, see Chapter II of this volume.

Sometimes the pupils presently served by an overaged school building may be served by adjacent school buildings of more modern design. Organizational flexibility, such as changes in the attendance area boundaries, combination of districts, removal of traffic hazards, or the use of temporary portable classrooms in areas of declining enrollment, may make it feasible to abandon an obsolete facility. There is little justification for spending a substantial amount of money to modernize even a thoroughly sound old structure if there will not be a long-term need for a school building at this general location.

Modernization or replacement.   The modernization or replacement of obsolete educational facilities is one of the most difficult decisions facing many school districts. Modernization is cheaper in initial cost (comprehensive modernization projects usually cost between one-third to one-half the cost of new school buildings of comparable capacity), yet most modernization projects result in structures that are considerably below new schools in their degree of educational adequacy. Recent stringent fire safety regulations have caused school districts throughout the nation to invest millions of dollars in old school buildings which are woefully inadequate for continued use. This major financial investment, designed to increase the safety of the building's occupants, has forced the continuation of obsolete and inadequate educational facilities far beyond their intended use. What to do with the old school building has become one of the most vexing problems confronting local school districts.

The New York State School Building Commission suggests twelve questions to guide the planner in deciding whether to modernize, replace, or abandon obsolete educational facilities. These questions are:

1. Will there be need for a school at this general location for an extended period of time?
2. Can the pupils be accommodated now or at some future time without modernizing or replacing the present building?
3. Is the site suitably located for continued school use?
4. Is the site sufficiently large? If not, can it be enlarged?
5. What deficiencies, if any, exist in the structure or its mechanical service systems?
6. Does the structure present insurmountable or serious obstacles to alteration, remodeling, and expansion where necessary?
7. What must be done to make the building conform to local health and safety codes?

8. What must be done to make the structure conform to minimum state or local educational space standards?
9. What would it cost to modernize the structure satisfactorily?
10. What would it cost to replace the building?
11. Would differences in educational space standards, periods of probable usefulness and subsequent costs of insurance, operation and maintenance, offset any immediate savings through modernization?
12. What other decisions have to be made?

The answers to the above questions outline a procedure which can be adapted to serve school districts of varying size. A negative answer to certain of the twelve questions may rule out over-all modernization of a building. However, it is possible to answer several of the questions in the negative and still decide to invest money in improving a structure.

A detailed analysis of the educational and structural adequacy of an existing school building is needed prior to the final decision on modernization or replacement. This analysis may best be made by a team of specialists including the building principal, head custodian, director of educational facilities planning, consulting architect, and structural engineer. A School Facility Obsolescence Survey Form has been developed to aid in the evaluation of obsolete educational facilities. The survey form includes a format and procedure for detailed evaluation of the following major categories of an obsolete facility:

1. Site
2. Building Structure
3. Heating and Ventilation
4. Fire Protection
5. Illumination
6. Electric Services
7. Toilets and Water Supply
8. Lockers and Storage
9. Classrooms
10. General Rooms
11. Administrative Room
12. Special Rooms[3]

2 State of New York Commission on School Buildings, *What To Do About Old School Buildings* (Albany, New York: The Commission, 1954), p. 5.

3 Donald Leu, Floyd Parker, and Kenneth Glass, *School Facility Obsolescence Survey Form* (East Lansing, Michigan: College of Education, Michigan State University, 1960).

This form was developed to assist in identifying the specific obsolete characteristics and the degree of obsolescence. Its use should insure a careful and complete evaluation of an obsolescent structure.

Cost of modernization versus replacement is of considerable importance in arriving at a final decision. The development of accurate cost estimates requires the preparation of a project plan listing the deficiencies to be corrected and the work to be done to bring the structure up to acceptable minimum standards. The following project plan outlines the needed modernization of one school building located in Minneapolis, Minnesota. It clearly illustrates the intensive modernization required in most school buildings constructed a half-century ago.

Franklin Junior High School was erected in 1874, rebuilt in 1917, and an addition was constructed in 1924. If this building is to be retained over a long period of time as a junior high school facility by the Minneapolis Public School system, it needs extensive modernization and rehabilitation in order to meet present standards of health, safety, and educational adequacy.

The classrooms should be rehabilitated to include additional storage, modern display boards, and furnishings. Many classrooms are of minimal size for a modern educational program. Needed improvements in the physical education area are increased gymnasium floor space, adequate storage, and modern locker and shower facilities. The industrial arts department needs renovation as well as adequate equipment and furnishings. A rehabilitated home economics suite is needed, including adequate storage and modern furnishings and equipment. An enlarged instructional materials center (library) is needed, with provisions made for teacher and librarian work areas, adequate shelving and storage, and modern equipment and furnishings.

The student lunchroom needs modernized furnishings and equipment. A teachers' lounge, including dining and restroom facilities should be provided. Inadequate plumbing facilities present a potential health hazard and should be repaired or replaced. An enlarged administrative suite is needed, including adequate space for general offices, health service, guidance center, and storage. A modern communication system should be installed.

To improve the physical environment within the building, the heating, ventilation, and temperature control system should be rehabilitated. Corridor, step, and floor repairs; acoustical tiling; plaster patching and painting; and window repairs are also necessary to improve the environment. The janitorial service requires an engineer's office, including toilet and shower and locker room facilities, as well as additional storage for equipment and supplies.

The appearance of the building's exterior and its surrounding site need improvement. An improved roof is needed. Additional off-street parking, landscaping, and improved play areas are needed, as well as fence, sidewalk and curb repairs. The 2.0 acre site is extremely small according to present-day standards for junior high school site adequacy; additional acreage should be acquired through cooperative effort with the Urban Renewal Program.[4]

The cost of the modernization project outlined above was estimated to be approximately 35 per cent less than the cost of a new facility of the same pupil capacity. The renovation, however, would result in a building containing less adequate educational spaces than a new building. The old building would be more costly to operate and maintain. The existing structure would not be properly located to serve its future service area. It would, therefore, represent false economy to recommend a comprehensive modernization of the school. The application of the questions and principles previously noted provided a clear answer to the complex question of modernization or replacement of obsolete educational facilities.

The Modernization Project

When the decision has been made to modernize a specific school building, the resultant question concerns the amount and type of modernization. The larger the fiscal investment in an older building the longer it must be continued in use in order to recapture the money invested. Unfortunately, some school districts have expended large sums of money on the modernization of overaged school buildings only to discover at a later date that the old school building does not belong in the school district's total long-term building program.

---

4 Donald J. Leu and John J. McNicholas, *Planning for the Future, Minneapolis Public Schools, Volume I* (East Lansing, Michigan: College of Education, Michigan State University, 1963), pp. 196–197.

If a school building does not constitute an integral part of the long-term plan, or if a comprehensive and costly modernization project results in a building containing largely inadequate educational spaces, it should not be modernized.

The approach to the problem of modernization involves four distinct steps:

1. The development of a long-term school building plan for the entire school district.
2. The evaluation of the overaged school building to determine whether it should be modernized or abandoned within the framework of a long-term plan.
3. The development of educational specifications designed to guide the architect in his design solution of the modernization project.
4. The completion of the modernization project.

The educational specifications should set forth philosophical as well as physical requirements for transforming an obsolete educational facility into a modern and functional school building. These specifications should give careful attention to city and state fire and safety requirements. The educational specifications designed for use in planning new school buildings may serve as a useful guide in modernizing older school facilities. It must be recognized, however, that it is financially unwise to attempt all of the design features of new construction in the modernization of an older school building. For example, older school buildings frequently contain classrooms of approximately 600 square feet of usable space. Bearing wall construction in these older buildings may make it prohibitively expensive to remove these walls in order to provide modern classrooms of 900 or more square feet. The unusual cost involved in bringing a school's heating system up to modern thermal standards is another example of cost compromises frequently adopted when modernizing an overaged school building. In fact many modernization projects may be described as a series of compromises leading to mediocrity and resulting in frequent curtailment of desired educational programs. It is desirable to hold down the cost of modernization to insure earlier abandonment of obsolete educational facilities. Schools and classrooms have changed dramatically in use and requirements during the past half-century. Recent major changes in the fabric of our society give clear indication that the rate and kind of change in American public education will increase during the next 50 years.

The following description of the use of one overaged classroom in a metropolitan city clearly illustrates the continuing change in the use of a typical classroom, "Room 103," during a period of 40 years.

Room 103 has been in existence through the tenure of five superintendents of schools, and it is in use during the tenure of the sixth superintendent. A total of five principals have assigned students and teachers to the room. A sixth principal is continuing to allocate space within the building, and Room 103 was partially utilized during the school year 1961–62. The records are incomplete, but since 1920 a partial list of the teachers and the grade levels or functions accommodated would include:

Year	Teacher	Use or Grade Level
1920–21	E. Robinson	2B, 2A, and 3B
1922	C. Starr	2A
1923	C. Neale	2A and 3B
1924	R. Sullivan	2A and 3B
1925	O. Stowell	3A
1926–27	M. VanLeuvin	4B and 4A
1928–29	R. Sullivan	2A
1930	A. Hont	2A
1931–32–33	C. Tuck	Special Education A
1934	M. Ryalls	Special Education A
1935	C. Tuck	Special Education A
1936		Used part-time as gym and for play classes and instrumental music
1937–38		Used part-time for instrumental music and four arithmetic classes per day
1939–50		Vacant
1951–57		Used as attendance center for the Southwest District of Detroit
1958		Used part-time as TV center
1959–60		Used as health room and TV center
1961–62		A teacher added to the staff and room returned to service as classroom

Room 103 has been used as a regular classroom for Grades 2 through 5 and a special education room for children with an age range of seven years (ages six to twelve). It has been used as a gymnasium or play room, an instrumental music room, and a business or attendance office. During the period of use as a classroom, as few as 20 pupils have been housed within its walls and as many as 53 have been in one class.[5]

"Room 103" indicates the continuing change in the use of a typical classroom. Actually, the classroom was woefully inadequate to efficiently serve any of its varied uses during the past 30 years. It would be exceedingly unwise to invest large sums of money into its modernization and thereby force its continued use for additional decades. If these older classrooms must be modernized, the planning should be designed to encourage early abandonment of the obsolete school. Careful planning makes it possible to modernize older classrooms inexpensively, with considerable flexibility, and still provide a quality teaching-learning atmosphere.

Flexibility.   Modernization projects should permit and encourage change in the use of each space. The predictions of any person involved in school plant planning may be based on the best available data and still may become useless within a few years. Shifting populations quickly affect space needs in school buildings. Abnormal economic and social conditions may create population explosions (in-migration), where hundreds of additional children are deposited on the steps of a school within a short time. On the other hand, it is entirely possible that industrial needs or expressway developments may reduce the need for a building in a short span of time. In either event, whether the population change occurs rapidly or slowly, it is entirely possible that buildings may become either overloaded or partially full or may need to be abandoned. Equipment (furniture, fixtures, other movable items) that can be readily deployed from room to room or building to building will result in educational and economic advantages.

Normally, the process of school plant modernization has included changes that re-equip and redesign the school for an additional 20 to 50 years of life. Perhaps such action should be taken if there is no doubt that the facility will be used for many years. However, if it is impossible to accurately predict future needs, it may be said that money is being wasted in the process of modernization.

Every year school administrators face problems in the assignment of students to classrooms made inadequate because the grade

[5] Donald J. Leu and Richard L. Featherstone, *Room 103, Deployable Space* (East Lansing, Michigan: Michigan State University, 1963), p. 8.

loads have shifted with little rhyme or reason. Administrators recognize the restrictions on education resulting from assigning sixth-grade students to second-grade rooms, or in using a general classroom for a specialized purpose. Where equipment is fixed or built in, few if any changes may be made. The occupants must continue to use improperly scaled equipment and fixtures. The truly flexible room, by the simple shifting of equipment and fixtures, will become functional regardless of the age level of the occupants. Room and equipment design should lend themselves to quick and efficient change from grade to grade, or from a general classroom to social studies or an art or science room. Such design possibilities free curriculum planners from the restrictions of obsolete facilities and provide for true flexibility in the use of space.

The following partial description of a modernization project for a typical obsolete classroom suggests various ways in which a room may be modernized to provide maximum flexibility, high standards of educational adequacy, and a minimum long-term dollar investment into the old school building.

Chalkboards and tackboards may be designed so that they may be easily raised or lowered to serve the changing age groups utilizing the classroom. This flexible design permits variation in the amount of chalkboard or tackboard, plus easy removal or replacement of the material used. Old hardwood floors may be refinished and sealed or covered with tile or carpet. Carpeting, for example, could serve a number of purposes: (1) acoustical floor rather than ceiling, (2) fuel savings, (3) environmental improvement, (4) covering of floor splinters and screw holes, and (5) use of material that may be deployed from room to room or building to building.

The window wall of the classroom may be improved by adding movable units such as sink and storage cabinets, bookcases, and a simple attractive screen to cover ugly exposed radiators. Draperies, controlling natural light, may be added over the blinds to darken the room for audiovisual purposes. Free standing storage and work cabinets along with colorful, modern, and movable furniture may replace the old fixed furniture. Repainting classrooms with pleasant pastel colors instead of the drab "school-house brown" is the most inexpensive way of improving the appearance of older classrooms. Younger children are especially stimulated by the careful use of combinations of yellows, reds, blues, greens, and pleasant pastel colors.

One of the major changes required in most overaged classrooms is in the lighting and acoustical treatment of the room. Most of these classrooms have no acoustical treatment and have antiquated lighting fixtures providing a low quantity of illumination along with excessive glare. Modern fluorescent lighting fixtures may be installed to provide sufficient quality and quantity of light to meet general classroom requirements. These fixtures may be designed and installed to permit their utilization in other school buildings at a future date. It is not necessary to provide acoustical materials covering the entire ceiling. Spots of acoustical treatment, especially in the corners of the classrooms, are usually adequate to control most sound problems. The use of easily removable "geocoustical" tile is another example of deployable improvements.

Flexible planning should include designs which permit and encourage a room to be changed in use from a classroom serving little children to a room serving young adults, or from a general classroom to a specialized instructional space. For example, the modernization project previously described could be converted from a classroom to an adequate art room by the following simple changes:

Removal
1 Bookcase
2 Clothing storage liners
2 Half-round tables
1 Free-standing storage cabinet
32 Table-desks

Addition
1 Combination sink and storage cabinet
2 Supply storage liners
1 Free-standing display cabinet
1 Kiln
1 Workbench
4 Work tables
2 Movable storage cabinets common to both rooms

The basic classroom could be easily changed to a general science classroom by removing the classroom furniture and equipment and adding the following items:

1 Combination sink and storage cabinet
2 Supply storage liners
1 Section chalkboard
5 Work tables

1 Portable demonstration sink
1 Teaching demonstration table
1 Free-standing display cabinet

It is significant to note that all of the listed equipment may be recovered from the school when and if the classroom or entire building is to be abandoned for educational purposes.

Cost of Modernization

It is unwise to state how much a specific school building modernization project will cost. New fire safety standards, for example, may double the estimated cost of a specific project. Comprehensive modernization projects of complete school buildings have frequently varied from one-third to one-half of the cost of new school construction. Actually, a modernization estimate must be developed for each area in the building. The following budget illustrates an estimate for converting one classroom into a modern, flexible, and deployable space:

Sand and refinish floors	$ 80.00
Remove existing chalkboards and trim; patch plaster; paint	225.00
Install hooks and clothing storage liners	100.00
Install radiator enclosures	120.00
Construct and install modular storage unit	284.00
Change double-acting doors	100.00
Purchase and install chalkboard and corkboards	225.00
Purchase and install ceiling units:	
Lights	950.00
Geocoustics	110.00
Furnishings:	1,118.75
Teacher's desk and chair	
32 tables and chairs	
3 bookcases	
2 half-round tables	
2 storage cabinets	
Total	$3,312.75

A large number of obsolete classrooms exist in every city in the United States. The school's name will be different, but the factors of educational obsolescence and structural soundness will be similar. All these classrooms will not and cannot be abandoned. It is financially impossible to abandon 50 per cent of our city schools. At the same time, it is unwise to invest large sums of money in a rehabilitation program when the building may be abandoned within a few years because of new expressways, urban renewal, etc. Community morale problems frequently arise when all the new buildings are built on the periphery of the city and the old facilities left to decay. Attempts must be made to provide equal building facilities as well as equal educational programs to all parts of the school district. In fact, these older facilities must meet the needs of a modern educational program. This chapter has suggested guidelines for the modernization of overaged, structurally sound, and educationally obsolete school buildings.[6]

---

[6] The author has drawn heavily from Donald J. Leu and Richard L. Featherstone, *Room 103, Deployable Space* for much of the material included in this section of the chapter.

CHAPTER V

Financing Capital Outlay Programs

The financing of school building construction is a difficult task facing all school districts. Finance is the universal tool of social and institutional control. Money, or lack of it, will control the way an organization is operated and managed. Schools and school buildings are no exception. In contemporary education nearly everything in the way of goods and services must be bought and paid for. It is an easy decision to continue the use of obsolete educational facilities by not providing needed financial resources; more difficult is the creation of major improvements in school buildings by acquiring additional revenue. From hiring the first teacher and purchasing the first book to constructing a new school or modernizing the old structure, finance is a critical determinant.

Throughout the United States there is a crucial shortage of quality school buildings. This shortage is most serious in our rapidly growing suburbs of limited financial resources and in our old, decaying "core" cities. Continuing high birth rates, increased population mobility, and a backlog of school construction resulting from the depression and war years have contributed to this shortage. A recent report from the U.S. Office of Education describes the school building situation thus:

The accumulated shortage of instruction rooms from past years remains high despite the fact that in the last six years (1955–56 through 1960–61) an annual average of 69,100 rooms were completed.[1]

Although 62,700 rooms are scheduled for completion in 1961–62, only a small part of the total can be applied against the reduction of the backlog of 127,000 rooms. This is due to the fact that thousands of rooms will be needed by the fall of 1962 to provide for population shifts, the estimated annual enrollment increase of over

---

[1] U.S. Department of Health, Education and Welfare, Office of Education, *Fall, 1961 Enrollment, Teachers and School Housing,* Circular No. 676 (Washington, D.C.: Government Printing Office, 1962), p. 6.

a million pupils, and replacements of rooms abandoned during the years for various reasons.[2]

The estimated annual increase of over one million pupils will require approximately two billion dollars per year to provide new school buildings. When this amount is added to the estimated backlog of 127,000 classrooms, and the continuing obsolescence of existing overaged school buildings, it becomes readily apparent that financing school construction is, and will continue to be, a multibillion dollar problem facing the citizens of our nation.

The expenditure of large sums of money for capital outlay programs should proceed in an orderly, carefully planned sequence. "Crash" programs of school construction are inherently wasteful and inefficient. Good planning requires thoughtful decisions by numerous educational, financial, and legal specialists. Prior to formulating a specific financial program, the long-term capital outlay needs of the district should be carefully developed. Normally a bond issue represents one step in achieving the recommended long-term building program.

Sources of Capital Outlay Monies

The three major sources of money for school construction are: local taxes, state support programs, and federal grants. Federal funds for school construction constitute a minor source of aid for most school districts. Most federal funds for education are paid to the state, rather than the local district, and are granted to encourage new or special programs. Vocational education, science equipment, guidance and counseling, and junior college support are examples of recent federal grants. It should be noted that federal funds for local noncapital outlay needs may free some existing local tax revenues for school construction purposes. In those areas of our nation where the federal government employs or houses large numbers of people, federal funds may be available for school construction. A careful investigation of the availability of federal funds should precede the planning and financing of school buildings. Frequently, a significant portion of the specialized equipment may be acquired through the utilization of available federal matching funds. Future years should witness an increased participation by our federal

---

[2] *Ibid.*

government in the fiscal solution of our nationwide school building problem.

Local property taxes provide the major source of current financing of school buildings. Historically, the United States has had local support in providing school buildings. Recent years have witnessed an increasing number of states participating in a wide variety of ways in the financing of school construction. The tremendous differences in rate of enrollment growth and local financial resources makes it impossible for many school districts to provide adequate educational facilities. This tradition of exclusive local responsibility in the financing of school buildings is one of the major barriers to achieving adequate educational facilities. Wealthy school districts have ample funds to finance quality school buildings for all their students. Financially poor school districts must frequently resort to prolonged use of unsafe, overcrowded, and inadequate facilities. Rapidly growing districts often are forced into half-day sessions for large portions of their students for extended periods of time. Obviously, we cannot move towards equal educational opportunities for all our children and youth without a partnership program of local, state, and federal support of education. This support program should include both the educational program and the educational facilities needed to house these children.

State Programs for School Construction

Alabama was the first state to provide state aid for school buildings. This plan, adopted by the legislative session of 1901, provided aid for rural school buildings. During the following 25 years a small number of southern states enacted legislation providing state monies and loans for rural school buildings, Negro schools, fiscally distressed districts, and as an incentive for school district reorganization. In 1927, Delaware began providing the major costs of school construction at the state level and required only a small local participation. A few states began to include capital outlay support in their emerging "foundation" programs. Following the end of World War II it became increasingly apparent that many local school districts could not by themselves solve their acute school building problems. Thus began the emergence of a wide variety of state support programs for school construction. Currently some 29 states are providing some type of assistance.

State grants.   State bonds have been issued to finance all or part of a program of direct state grants in a number of states, including South Carolina, Delaware, Vermont, and Washington. These states have used their general credit to borrow money for school purposes and have allocated the money to local school districts.

Another group of states has insisted that local school districts use their own borrowing capacity and issue their own bonds without the aid of state bond issues. These states, however, have been liberal in giving assistance to the districts to meet debt service payments on their bonds.

In Massachusetts, for example, annual appropriations are made from the state's general revenues to directly finance state grants for school construction. The grants may be used in two ways. Either the state gives funds directly to the district towards the cost of school construction, or, if the bonded indebtedness exceeds more than 50 per cent of the cost of the project, the amount of the grant is divided by the number of years the indebtedness will remain outstanding, and the grant paid in equal annual installments during a period in which the bonds are being retired. Connecticut has a somewhat similar program using state general funds.[3]

The state of Washington has an equalizing matching plan in which the state provides between 25 per cent and 90 per cent of the school building costs. A limitation of the Washington plan is, however, its emphasis on meeting emergency needs rather than the continuing needs of the local school districts.

State bond issues for loans.   California, Maryland, and Michigan are examples of states which use the state's borrowing power to assist local school districts. Under the Michigan plan a district qualifying for a state loan may issue bonds for a period of 25, but not more than 30 years. These bonds are not subject to the 15 mill taxing limitation present on limited tax bonds. Bonds issued under this plan require only a vote of the tax-paying electors to bond the district for a specific amount of money. Since the bonds are unlimited tax bonds, the local board of education has the authority to set the necessary tax rate for debt retirement each year. A school

---

[3] *The Cost of a Schoolhouse* (New York: The Educational Facilities Laboratories, Inc., 1960), pp. 123–24.

district may limit its tax rate for the retirement of qualified tax bonds to 13 mills on the state equalized valuation of the district, and any additional amount needed to meet the payment of principal and interest on qualified bonds may be borrowed from the state.

Under the California plan the provisions for repayment of a school district loan are such that the district is not required to make any repayment to the state in a year when the district's total levy to meet prior bonded debt is 4 mills. However, if a 3 mill levy ($3.00 per $1,000 local valuation) will meet prior bonded debt in that year, the district is required to repay the state an amount equal to a 1 mill levy. State loans in California must be paid off in 30 years and any debt unpaid at the end of 30 years is automatically written off by the state.

It should be understood that the plans utilized in California, Maryland, and Michigan are loans from the states and not grants. This type of assistance is not part of a foundation program designed to equalize fiscal ability. The major advantages of a Michigan-type loan program are as follows:

1. Districts experiencing rapid growth may, with the state's assistance, bond and build school buildings to house their mushrooming school enrollments.
2. Less wealthy districts may provide needed educational facilities if their taxpayers will vote the relatively high milleage.
3. The "full faith and credit" of the state in support of the bonds tends to result in lower interest rates.
4. School district reorganization is encouraged by not qualifying bonds for school districts which should be consolidated.

Other types of state aid.   Some states have revolving loan funds for aid to local districts. These funds are set up with monies from current revenues, special appropriations, or other sources exclusive of bond issues. Arkansas has such a fund from which it grants small loans, the maximum being $50,000 to any one district.

Virginia's loan fund, also known as the "State Literary Fund," has been used by most of the districts which have let contracts for school construction since 1950. Loans of up to 100 per cent of the cost of construction have been made with relatively low interest rates. Annual repayments on the principal are made for a period of 30 years. Under this arrangement more than $36 million was committed to school districts in the years between 1950 and 1957.[4]

---

[4] *The Cost of a Schoolhouse, op. cit.,* p. 123.

In 1958 New Jersey authorized a fund to be used to purchase a school district bond issue when a default is anticipated, or to pay interest on such bonds in the hands of outside holders so long as the district is unable to make such payments. Although this fund is relatively small, totaling only $18 million in 1958, it definitely has been a strengthening factor for marginal school district bonds of that state.[5]

New York also has recently provided a new type of state aid program for school building bonds. This measure gives relief to certain school districts which are compelled to pay an excessive interest rate on their bonds. School districts are eligible for such aid if the rate of interest they must pay is more than one-fourth of 1 per cent in excess of the average rate paid on similar bond maturities by those districts which sold bonds during the previous six months. Many districts which receive other types of school building aid are ineligible for excessive interest aid.[6]

State support for school construction is nonexistent in some states and of limited value in others. No state has yet provided a comprehensive capital outlay program which will insure quality educational facilities for all its students. Morphet and Reller have provided considerable leadership by their development of suggested criteria or characteristics of a sound program of state support for capital outlay needs. These criteria, developed over a decade ago, provide excellent guidelines for evaluating existing and proposed programs. The criteria are as follows.

General Guidelines:

1. Each state should make provision for state participation in the financing of capital outlay programs.
2. The state program for financing capital outlay should be developed through sound, comprehensive studies.
3. An acceptable program should provide adequately and equitably for all essential school plant needs.
4. The state plan should provide for both emergency and long-range needs.
5. All districts should be eligible to participate in accordance with needs.

---

[5] *Ibid.*, p. 124.
[6] *Ibid.*, p. 124.

Guidelines pertaining to Finance:

1. The state plan for financing capital outlay should be developed as an integral part of the foundation program of education.
2. Provision should be made in the program for state grants or grants and loans rather than for loans alone.
3. The program should be financed through an equitable combination of state and local revenue.
4. Funds for the program should be derived chiefly from current state revenues and insofar as practical from current local revenues.
5. An objective formula for apportioning funds should be included in the law.
6. The program should provide for equitable local tax effort.
7. Each local school system should have a reasonable margin of local tax leeway and bonding ability.

Guidelines to Administration.

1. The program should be administered by the state department of education.
2. The program should place maximum emphasis on local responsibility and state leadership.
3. Comprehensive local school plant studies should be required.
4. Each local school system should develop and adopt a long-range program.
5. The state program should assure that all necessary facilities can be provided at permanent school centers.
6. Building plans and specifications should be submitted to the state department of education for checking as to conformity to a few broad minimum standards.
7. Except for funds provided strictly for emergency programs, districts should be permitted to use capital outlays funds provided through the program either during the current year or to place such funds on deposit so they can be accumulated over a reasonable period of years and used as needed.
8. The basic state and local capital outlay funds should be required to be used for bona fide capital outlay purposes or for debt service under certain conditions.[7]

State support programs for school construction have been evolving during the past half-century. The majority of the 50 states now have some form of state assistance for school buildings. Loans, grants, and other forms of financial assistance are becoming more

---

[7] Edgar L. Morphet and Theodore L. Reller, *State Provisions for Financing Public School Capital Outlay Costs,* Field Service Leaflet No. 1 (Berkeley: University of California, Department of Education, 1952).

common each year as local districts find it increasingly difficult to provide adequate educational facilities for their children and youth. Colleges and universities are now beginning to face the school construction crisis resulting from rapidly increasing school enrollments. This year witnessed the passage of a federal loan program to aid in the construction of educational facilities for institutions of higher learning. However, no real solution is in sight for the majority of our local school districts. A partnership program of local, state, and federal support seems to offer the only real long-term solution to this crucial problem.

Methods of Payment

Paying for needed school construction is a complex problem which faces all school districts. Few districts possess enough wealth or enrollment stability to pay cash for their school buildings. The four methods available from local resources are: (1) pay-as-you-go (current revenues), (2) savings, through the use of a capital reserve fund, (3) borrowed money, or (4) a combination of the three methods. The selection of the most desirable method requires careful consideration of the fiscal characteristics of the local district, its total building needs, and the availability of outside financial assistance. Careful design of a fiscal plan may result in considerable economy to the district.

Pay-as-you-go. Because of limited state support, along with constitutional and statutory limitations on the local tax rate, most school districts need all of their current tax receipts to meet operating expenses. A pay-as-you-go plan (current revenues) normally requires the voting of an additional annual tax to be used for building purposes. Unfortunately some districts have been forced to divert needed operating monies to capital outlay projects. A pay-as-you-go program is ordinarily successful only in a district with a considerable taxable wealth, or in a district with limited capital outlay needs. A relatively wealthy school district with limited school building needs recurring every two or three years has less reason to resort to long-term borrowing than other districts. It should be noted, however, that most large cities have incurred such a large backlog of obsolete educational facilities that their building problems can seldom be solved by this method of financing.

To illustrate the cost of long-term financing to such a district, assume that it has annual capital outlay needs of $1,000,000 for which it issues thirty-year bonds each year at 3.2 per cent interest and with equal annual principal payments. For the first several years, annual carrying charges would be less than $1,000,000, but in the thirtieth year and every year thereafter it would be paying $1,000,000 on its old bonds plus $496,000 in interest, or a total of $1,496,000 for each $1,000,000 of construction. In addition, after the thirtieth year the district would always have an indebtedness of $14,500,000. Thirty million dollars worth of school buildings would cost nearly $45,000,000 if financed by thirty-year 3.2 per cent bonds. If this district paid for its school construction without borrowing, it would reduce its annual and total capital outlay expenditures by about a third and have no outstanding debt at any time.[8]

The advantages of using current revenues and short maturity schedules in financing capital programs in districts with constant needs have been summarized by the New York State Commission on School Buildings as follows.

1. More money can be saved.
2. More schools can be built for the same money or more funds are available for the educational program and other government services in districts not up to their tax limit.
3. The board has greater freedom in adapting methods of payment to changes in economic conditions, since borrowing power is conserved.
4. The board is better equipped financially to meet extraordinary building needs and to level off debt service requirements.[9]

Savings (capital reserve funds). This method of finance is frequently called the building and site sinking fund. It is actually a variation of the pay-as-you-go plan of financing. Under this plan the receipts from a special tax or diversions from existing monies are set aside in a sinking fund until sufficient monies have been accumulated to pay for the proposed construction. This fund is frequently established by the school district for a specific school building project or site acquisition and for a definite amount to

8 *More Schools for Your Money* (Albany, New York: State of New York Commission on School Buildings, 1954), p. 14.
9 *Ibid.,* p. 15.

be accumulated over a certain number of years. Prior to expending the accumulated funds the money is frequently invested and interest is accumulated.

The major advantages claimed for this method of financing school construction are:

1. Reductions of the amount needed to be borrowed at some future time, and consequent reductions in total interest costs.
2. Reduction in interest rates on what borrowing is done, because of improved credit.
3. Extension of payments over a period longer than the legal period of probable usefulness of the project, if this is desirable or necessary.
4. Distributing taxes for capital expenses more evenly over the years, because, when taxes for debt service are low or nonexistent, reserve funds can be created to avoid later periods of high taxes for debt service.[10]

It should be noted that school districts have utilized capital reserve funds to purchase school sites far in advance of their actual needs. This procedure has made it possible to secure sites of adequate size and proper location at a considerable saving in cost to the school district. One rapidly growing suburban school district, for example, has estimated a total savings of approximately three million dollars by the early acquisition of five school sites totaling 174 acres.[11]

Borrowing.   The large majority of school districts find it necessary to finance school building construction through the issuing of bonds. School bonds may be compared with the mortgage a homeowner takes out to finance the purchase of his new home. School bonds, however, are not secured by a mortgage on the school building, but are general obligations for which the full faith, credit, and taxing power of the school district are pledged as security. A few states in order to achieve better marketability of the bonds and lower interest rates "back up" the local district by pledging the faith and credit of the state to state approved bond issues. In order to pay the annual costs of the issued bonds the school district must appropriate enough to pay principal and interest. If the district should fail to do so, it may be directed to set aside for the purpose of payment the first tax money the district receives.

[10] *Ibid.,* p. 9.
[11] *The Cost of a Schoolhouse, op. cit.,* pp. 46–47.

The income derived from school district bonds are tax-exempt to the bond owner. This tax-exempt feature facilitates their sale in competition with higher yield corporate bonds and other investment opportunities and it permits school districts to finance school construction at a comparatively low cost. A second reason for the low interest rates found in school bonds is the relative security of school bonds. Seldom, throughout the United States, has a school district defaulted on bond payments. This historical security of investment has made school bonds most attractive in the bond market.

The four types of districts who typically borrow funds for school construction are (1) school districts experiencing rapid growth, (2) newly consolidated districts, (3) districts of limited wealth, and (4) districts with a large backlog of obsolete educational facilities.

Rapidly growing districts find it extremely difficult to do accurate long-term planning or to predict and control surges of new enrollment. They are usually swamped with young families having large numbers of school-age children. School needs must be met before industrial and commercial property appears on the tax rolls. These conditions weaken the credit rating of the school district and tend to increase interest rates on school bonds.

During the last several decades, the reorganization of small inefficient school districts into larger educational units has been taking place throughout the United States. This reorganization usually results in the immediate need for a new comprehensive high school and a number of larger elementary schools. Frequently the primary motive for consolidation is the acute need of new school buildings throughout the area. The fiscal problems of reorganized school districts are quite similar to the problems of rapidly growing districts. These new districts have not yet had the opportunity to complete their long-term planning or to establish sinking funds for future capital outlay needs. The financing of school construction requires a large initial tax burden. Boards of education in reorganized districts may consider it advisable to provide for bonds featuring long maturity schedules of repayment. The establishment of a high initial credit rating is most important for any new district.

School districts of limited financial resources located in states providing inadequate state fiscal support represent a tragic chapter in American educational history. These districts represent a poor risk to bond investors and therefore must borrow at relatively high interest rates. A significant portion of their inadequate financial resources must be diverted to paying high interest on frequent borrowings. Frequently the educational program is "short-changed" in order to provide cheap and inadequate educational facilities.

Recent years have witnessed an increased awareness of the major capital outlay needs facing our largest cities. Years of neglect coupled with the in-migration of large numbers of lower socioeconomic families have compounded the problem. The average age of over half of their school buildings is between 40 and 50 years. This tremendous backlog of obsolete educational facilities should be immediately replaced. Surprisingly, many of these cities have been gaining in public school enrollments while losing in total population. A large percentage of their school buildings are located in the "core" of the city away from their shifting school-age populations. The acquisition of needed new sites in these cities is prohibitively expensive. New and expensive special facilities such as technical education, junior colleges, and special education facilities are desperately needed. The population is aging and less willing and less able to vote needed monies. New federal freeways, primarily designed to serve the nonresident commuters, are cutting into logical school attendance areas. Borrowing of money for needed new school buildings is only a small and partial answer to their capital outlay needs. These districts must borrow money in an attempt to erase a portion of their antiquated school plants. Pay-as-you-go plans are also needed to attempt to arrest further deterioration of school buildings. Massive programs of local, state, and federal support seem to offer the only realistic solution to their worsening capital outlay needs.

Some states have attempted to reduce the amount of borrowing by local districts for capital outlay needs by the creation of "building authorities." Under this plan, a separate and independent authority is created for the purpose of financing and constructing needed school buildings. The "authority" then leases the building to the local school district. Actually the building authority plan represents a way of avoiding antiquated constitutional and statutory debt limitations imposed upon local districts. This plan has been utilized with variations in Kentucky, Pennsylvania, Georgia, Indiana, Maine, and Wisconsin. A basic problem of this plan is that the least wealthy districts cannot afford to meet the rental payments without curtailing their operating programs.

There is no one fiscal plan that can best meet the capital outlay needs of a wide variety of school districts. Most school districts utilize a combination of two or more methods of finance. Careful long-term planning will result in considerable savings to the district and insure more adequate school buildings for its children and youth. A few states have moved vigorously toward establishing a sound partnership plan of fiscal support. No state has yet adopted a totally adequate capital outlay program as an integral part of the state "foundation" program. This lack of adequate state plans has forced large amounts of borrowing by local school districts with the resultant loss of needed local tax money to pay the interest charges on their loans.

Passing the Bond Issue

Careful planning for needed educational facilities is of little value if the citizens will not provide the needed fiscal support. Thus the successful passage of a school building bond issue is a necessary step in most building programs. Most educators are poor politicians. In fact the word "politics" is repugnant to many educators. This general reluctance on the part of educators primarily stems from our tradition of keeping partisan politics out of educational issues. The avoidance of partisan politics is good and necessary in American public education. The avoidance of recognizing politics as the science of government can be disastrous to our schools. The quality of education is frequently the result of the political skill of the educational leader.

There is no simple formula for insuring the successful passage of a needed bond issue. In the final analysis votes cast for or against a bond issue reflect the community's aspiration level for education, their understanding of the educational needs of the district, their confidence or lack of confidence in the school board and administrative staff, and their willingness to exercise their voting responsibility under our form of representative government. Bond issues have been passed by wide margins in school districts which have presented very limited public information programs. Conversely, many districts have waged an intensive public relations campaign only to have the issue defeated by a large majority of the voters.

Obviously, the short-term campaign preceding a bond issue vote represents only a small portion of activities required to pass a bond election. Some educators have falsely concluded that successful bond issues result from many large group meetings, massive communications, and a large voter turnout. "What happened?" is a frequent response to naive assumptions concerning the educational desires of those local citizens casting their votes.

The long-term plan. A carefully developed long-term plan of school building needs is a first step in passing any bond issue. Voters resist and resent stopgap planning which has been hurriedly and haphazardly conceived to meet short-term emergencies. The first short-term plan may be approved by the voters only to have them later discover that it is only a partial solution. Frequently these plans are discovered to be barriers to achieving long-term solutions. For example, one district expended $400,000 in the modernization and rehabilitation of an obsolete school building only to discover at a later date that this building did not logically belong as a part of the long-term plan. Voter confidence was shattered and a future bond issue was soundly defeated.

This long-term plan should be developed in cooperation with other units of government, civic organizations, and interested lay citizens. Lay citizens, however, should not be asked to serve as technical specialists in areas outside of their competence. And citizens should not be asked to determine the school building needs of the district when their true task is to assist in the passage of the bond issue. There is nothing wrong in asking interested citizens to assist in the passage of a bond issue; however, it is unethical and unwise to attempt to deceive them as to what their real task is. Citizen advisory organizations may be formed to assist in studying educational needs, and similar organizations may be created by the board of education for passing bond issues. Each of these advisory groups should have a clear understanding of their roles, responsibilities, and limitations.

The communication and interpretation of the long-term plan is a difficult task for school administrators. Most school building reports are lengthy and complex. The majority of the lay public cannot be expected to read such reports. Summary brochures utilizing simple visual illustrations is one effective technique of informing the public. Local newspapers, radio, and television stations may assist in running serial or spot articles on the school building needs. P.T.A.s often devote several programs in each neighborhood school for a review of the recommended program. Slides and other visual aids should be prepared for the association's use. Civic organizations will frequently devote time for a discussion of the needed educational facilities and often form subcommittees to study the educational needs in considerable detail and to make recommendations to their total membership. These study committees of civic organizations are becoming increasingly important in our larger cities. Frequently they are provided a substantial budget and professional staff and are designed to serve as "watch-dog" committees on public expenditures. Their involvement and support is of considerable importance in passing a bond issue.

Any recommended bond issue should be considered as a single step in achieving a long-term plan. Carefully communicated long-term planning pays large dividends in gathering public understanding and support.

The power structure concept.   At one time in the training of school administrators, considerable attention was given to the study of the power structure concept. Under this older concept of political force a community was diagrammed in terms of a single pyramid of decision-making powers. The task of the chief school administrator was to identify, join, and manipulate those few community leaders who controlled the major decisions. This concept, however, ignores the complex operational structure of our form of representative government and democratic school administration. Actually it assumes continuous control of the majority of the citizens by a stable power elite. Secondly, it is an oversimplified and erroneous concept of political decision-making. Some school leaders have attempted to climb this pyramid of power only to discover that the peak keeps shifting and vanishing. If there are decision-making centers in a local community, they may be more accurately described as a host of expanding, contracting, and overlapping nodules of interest and spheres of influence. A truly democratic society would theoretically and ideally be conceptualized as a flat line of power with every citizen having an equal voice in those decisions affecting him. Actually our form of representative government recognizes the legitimacy and necessity of giving elected and appointed officials

clearly defined responsibilities and decision-making powers. One
recent publication makes the following pertinent observation:

> Recent studies of political behavior call the rationality-activist
> model into question, for it is becoming clear that citizens in
> democracies rarely live up to this model. They are not well informed,
> not deeply involved, not particularly active; and the process by
> which they come to their voting decision is anything but a process
> of rational calculation.[12]

The concepts outlined above have obvious implications for the
passing of a bond issue or for the making of any educational decision affecting the citizens of a school district. Facts and information
concerning school building needs should be complete, accurate,
and available to all. Broad citizen participation is desirable and
necessary in American public education. Final control of local
public education resides in the lay public through their vote and
their elected lay boards of education.

Democratic leadership, which involves the affected individuals
in decision-making, should not be confused with laissez-faire administration. As the chief executive officer of the school board,
the superintendent of schools should direct the bond issue campaign.
He needs to recognize and involve key individuals and organizations. He should accurately identify and utilize community leaders.
The educational leader will need to anticipate those forces opposing increased expenditures for education and to prepare clear answers to their hard questions. His central task in the campaign is to
identify and utilize all of the available human resources willing to
assist in the improvement of education.

The "one-to-one" campaign.   Large public meetings, mass communication techniques, editorials, and public pronouncements of
support for the bond issue by community leaders and organizations
are necessary and desirable in any bond issue campaign, for these
standard techniques establish the underlying climate of community
support for the improvement of education. It should be recognized,
however, that these methods do not change a large percentage of
the vote, nor do these techniques of large group involvement cause
many individuals to leave their firesides and televisions to trudge

---

[12] Gabriel A. Almond and Sidney Yerba, *The Civic Culture* (Princeton, New
Jersey: Princeton University Press, 1963), p. 474.

through wind and snow to cast their individual vote. The single most effective method of passing a difficult bond issue is the "one-to-one" technique.

The one-to-one campaign borrows and adapts a method developed and utilized by political parties in their election of party candidates. It is the reverse of large mass meeting methods in that it originates with each individual in the school district. A volunteer "block leader" is recruited for each city block, and city blocks are organized into neighborhoods which normally conform to neighborhood elementary school attendance areas. Neighborhoods are then organized into natural communities, usually centering around a senior high school. A number of communities represent the total school district and are represented by the central citizens' committee for the passage of the bond issue. This central citizens' committee also coordinates the activities of various civic organizations committed to supporting the bond issue.

The individual voter and the block leader are the key individuals. The block leader is well informed of the school building needs and understands the fiscal implications. He is the individual responsible for informing his neighbors on the impending vote and asking their support. He is the two-way communication link between the individual citizen and the school district. Frequently, his work represents the difference between success and failure in a difficult bond issue. Transportation to the polls, babysitting service, and a personal reminder to vote on the day of the election are all methods utilized by these block leaders to help voters get to the polls. Block leaders spend little of their time on those individuals strongly committed for or against the bond issue. Their major assistance is directed to the uninformed, misinformed, or undecided voter. Another vital role performed by the block leader is to inform the central citizens' committee of the major concerns and unanswered questions of individual citizens and to provide clear answers to these difficult questions.

Some educators and citizens have voiced objections to the use of sophisticated political techniques in resolving issues concerning public education. Their objections are primarily concerned with insuring the separation of public education from partisan politics. This valid concern must be carefully considered by each local school district. Other objections, however, are voiced by some individuals opposing any increased expenditures for the improvement of education. These opponents of public education would prefer an amateur approach to the bond issue by school officials and condone the use of smear, fear, and misinformation by those against the issue. It should be noted that citizens actively participating in the passage of a bond issue are volunteers giving freely of their own time to assist in the improvement of education. Any resultant educational gains will be derived by the children and youth of the community and not by the involved citizens and educators. Secondly, the primary task of the educational leader is to attempt to improve education in the district. Thirdly, the final control of the kind and quality of public education in America rests with the individual citizen through his vote and his elected board of education. Citizen involvement in a bond issue is much preferred by the writer to the frequent technique of having the children carry home brochures which they do not understand.

Continuing responsibilities. The educational leader's responsibility to the citizens of his district does not cease with the successful passage of the bond issue. A favorable vote represents a vote of confidence in education as a worthy social and economic investment of tax dollars. Responsibility to each citizen accompanies their confidence in education. The taxpayer must be assured that tax dollars are not being wasted. New schools and improvements to existing buildings must be carefully planned and constructed. Progress reports on these schools should be made available to the general public. Questions concerning individual school buildings merit careful answers. One of the most difficult but most important tasks is to illustrate in simple language how the new school buildings contribute to the improvement of education for the children of the school district. Future votes reflect the citizens' satisfaction or dissatisfaction with the conduct of a previous school construction program.

Selling School Bonds

After the bond issue has been passed the local board of education is ready to begin preparation for the advertising of bids for sale of the bonds. Securing the lowest possible interest rate is of considerable importance to the school district. Borrowing adds substantially to the hidden cost of a school building. For example, a thirty-year

$10,000,000 bond issue costs over $16,500,000 to retire at an interest rate of 4 per cent. A 1 per cent increase in the interest rate adds another $1,600,000 in interest to the cost.

The Educational Facilities Laboratories makes the following suggestions to insure getting the most for school bond money:

1. Advertise. Let the investment field know who you are by printing a prospectus. A knowledge of your assets and future growth helps to convince potential buyers that your community is a safe place to invest their money.
2. If you're thinking of making a short-term loan to outride a high money market, unless you have a very clear crystal ball, think twice. The short-term issue can be a ghost that comes back to haunt you—it may carry you into a period of the highest interest rates ever.
3. Gear your bonds to appeal to the broadest group of buyers. Serial bonds do this best—they attract both long- and short-term investors.
4. Don't sell your bonds until you need the money. Schoolhouse construction is often a slow process. Let the architects complete the plans, let the bids be taken, let construction awards be made, before you sell your bonds. It can cost you a full year's additional interest if the bonds are outstanding a year too soon.
5. Watch your timing. Don't put your bonds up for sale when the market is glutted. Wait for the day or week when there are few other school issues for buyers to choose from.
6. Analyze the bids. If there aren't enough of them, or if they all seem too high, you might be wise to withdraw the issue, rework it, and offer it for sale another time.
7. Eliminate unnecessary legal costs. Since you will have to retain outside legal counsel who are specialists in the field of municipal bond law, there is no point in paying your local attorney an extra fee for the preparation of the bond proceedings. When the bond counselors are retained to render their opinion, they will prepare all the necessary papers without additional cost.
8. Make certain your bank pays you the going rate of interest on the money you receive from the sale of the bonds—or invest the proceeds in short-term U.S. government securities. Much of your bond money may be in the bank for several years while the schoolhouse is being built. Make that money work for your district.
9. Investigate your state's school construction aid program carefully so you can take advantage of all its benefits.[13]

---

[13] *The Cost of a Schoolhouse, op. cit.,* p. 125.

Preparing bond retirement schedules. The bond retirement schedule should be designed to enhance the salability of the bonds while conforming to local tax limitations and community fiscal desires. Short-term issues save interest but require higher tax payments. Over a quarter of a million dollars in interest charges may be saved by reducing a thirty-year $1,500,000 bond issue at 3.2 per cent to a twenty-year maturity schedule. Each bond issue, however, should be designed as an integral part of all previous bonds and anticipated future issues.

In developing and evaluating any fiscal plan the following criteria may be utilized. A capital outlay fiscal plan should

> . . . contribute to the orderly achievement of the long-term school building program.
> . . . provide adequate funds for the accomplishment of the recommended initial steps in the building program.
> . . . comply with a rule of repayment in the desired number of years.
> . . . not be in excess of existing statutory or constitutional debt limitations.
>
> . . . possess "open-end" compatibility for extension to succeeding stages of the long-term program.
> . . . be salable to the bond market.
> . . . enhance the credit rating of the school district.
> . . . contribute to an annual stability of total taxes paid by local citizens.

The local taxpayer is seldom interested in the complexities and details of a bond issue. He is, in fact, easily confused by repayment schedules, bonded indebtedness computations, and annual milleage rates required to retire the bond issue. His primary concern, expressed in simple language, is, "How much will this bond issue increase the annual tax bill on my home?" It is most helpful to summarize the fiscal plan in a table illustrating how much the bond issue will cost individuals owning homes of varying values (see Table 10).

Table 10 illustrates three possible ways of retiring a $24,000,000 bond issue (ten–, fifteen–, or twenty-year retirement plans). The ten-year retirement plan would cost an owner of a $15,000 house an average of $7.75 per year in taxes. The twenty-year plan would average $5.29 per year in additional taxes. Similar tables may be prepared for homes of higher or lower value. It is sometimes useful

TABLE 10

ANNUAL TAX BILL FOR $15,000 PROPERTY OWNER TO
RETIRE $24,000,000 VOTED BOND ISSUE *

Year	Ten-Year Retirement Plan	Fifteen-Year Retirement Plan	Twenty-Year Retirement Plan
1963	– – –	– – –	– – –
1964	– – –	– – –	– – –
1965	$ 1.78	$ .92	$ .92
1966	3.77	2.10	1.86
1967	6.31	3.28	2.69
1968	8.72	4.98	3.50
1969	11.07	6.73	4.31
1970	10.92	7.32	4.19
1971	11.51	7.80	4.86
1972	11.47	8.25	5.54
1973	11.41	8.05	6.44
1974	9.48	7.88	7.32
1975	7.20	8.18	7.91
1976	4.73	8.47	7.98
1977	2.34	8.75	7.73
1978		9.02	7.59
1979		7.57	7.38
1980		5.61	7.18
1981		3.68	6.99
1982		1.82	7.03
1983			6.82
1984			5.45
1985			4.02
1986			2.65
1987			1.30
Total	$ 100.71	$ 110.41	$ 121.66
Avg.	7.75/yr. for 13 yrs.	6.13/yr. for 18 yrs.	5.29/yr. for 23 yrs.

* Source: Donald J. Leu and John J. McNicholas, *Planning for the Future, Minneapolis Public Schools* (East Lansing, Michigan: College of Education, Michigan State University, 1963), p. 82.

to translate these tax schedules into daily tax costs. In the illustration, for example, the tax bill for the new building program could be converted to less than two cents a day in increased taxes for the average homeowner.

Marketing school bonds. The financial market provides a meeting place for the buyer and seller of school bonds. This market is similar to grain, produce, and other markets. Supply and demand, world and national economic conditions, federal policies, along with estimates of the future, affect the school bond market. Long-term interest rate trends are broken by short-term variations. Most educators are not at home in this complex market place and must rely on expert counsel by recognized specialists.

School bonds represent approximately one-third of all municipal bonds being offered in the financial market. The most important factor in marketing bonds is the credit rating of the local school district. These credit ratings are established by national credit rating agencies. Moodys Investors Service, on a rating scale starting with "Aaa," generally rates school bonds as "Aa," "A," and "Baa." Bonds rated the highest normally result in lower interest rates. Standard and Poors' Corporation, another major rating service, applies quality symbols which for school bonds range from "A1" and "A" to "B1+." Dunn and Bradstreet compiles a confidential credit reporting service when requested. In the case of school bonds, the bond dealer buys the entire issue of bonds from the district and sells the bonds to investors. A district's credit rating reflects the credit rater's evaluation of the school district's ability to repay their financial obligations.

Investors, prior to purchasing bonds, carefully examine the fiscal history and ability of the local school district. Typically investors consider such factors as:

1. Amount and maturity schedules of outstanding indebtedness of the district and other units of government serving the same area.
2. Immediate and future capital needs of the district and the area.
3. Revenue needs and tax levies for operating expenses of the district and the area.
4. Record of bond and interest payments and reserve funds.
5. Property and local nonproperty tax and debt burden.
6. Record of tax collections.
7. State aid in meeting operating expenses and building costs.
8. Population and population trends.
9. Assessed and full valuation of real estate in the district.
10. Income or wealth of the residents and its stability.
11. Number of children to be educated.
12. Diversity of and outlook for local industry.
13. Transportation facilities aiding business in the area.
14. Economic and social trends in the area.[14]

It is important that credit agencies be requested to provide a credit rating or report. This is provided at no charge to the district and is

[14] *More Schools for Your Money* (Albany, New York: State of New York Commission on School Buildings, 1954), pp. 22–23.

paid for by the investor. The school district should provide the credit agency with all the information requested and should add any information which they believe will enhance the school district's credit.

Bond issues should be advertised locally and in such national publications as *The Wall Street Journal* and *The Bond Buyer*. The principal sources for financing new schools are local banks and financial centers located in New York, Chicago, San Francisco, and Los Angeles.

A school board should select their bond attorney before taking any steps which may affect the issuance of its bonds. He is hired on a fee basis to give professional opinion with respect to the legality of a bond issue. Such opinions are required by national dealers and investors. He prepares papers and reviews procedures affecting the salability of bonds, expedites borrowing, advises on meeting technicalities, and furnishes appropriate forms. A careful distinction should be made between the functions of a qualified bond attorney and those of local legal counsel.[15]

Timing bond sales.   Varying interest costs on bonds are the resultant of marketability and timing. The three major factors involved in the timing of bonds are: (1) availability of funds in the market, (2) when the district needs the funds to construct their school buildings, and (3) anticipated changes in future interest rates. School districts should avoid placing their offerings on the market at the same time as other school districts with the same or similar names. Investors, with limited information, hesitate to buy when there is any confusion between the bonds of districts with similar names.

Some districts have utilized short-term loans when faced with an apparent temporary period of high interest rates. This "guessing" game has been proven costly to some school districts. Once short-term financing has been used, it usually cannot be repeated. Too much short-term debt tends to reduce the financial position of the district. Frequently short-term notes must be refinanced at higher interest rates. It is difficult to explain to local citizens and civic organizations the "gamblers loss" of a local board of education. If the bids on a long-term issue appear to be unusually high and if competent specialists advise against accepting these bids, it may be sound policy to reject the bids and re-offer the bonds at a later sale.

---

[15] *Ibid.*, p. 26.

This delay, however, may also prove costly to the district if interest rates continue to rise. Moreover, delay in construction of needed new educational facilities may result in increased construction costs which can offset any possible savings in interest.

CHAPTER VI

A Look into the Future

Winston Churchill is reported as remarking, "We shape our buildings, but thereafter they shape us." This statement is especially true of school buildings. Desired improvements in educational programs are frequently modified, restricted, or prohibited by the physical structure.

Major changes in society have far-reaching implications for the educational programs designed to serve this society. For example, automation and resultant job displacement, along with concomitant requirements for scientists, engineers, and highly-skilled technicians obviously place increased demands on our schools. The large-scale migration of citizens of lower socioeconomic groups to our central cities is creating new demands for changing educational programs. Periodic and regional recessions, with the unemployed being largely the poorly educated, have made clear the need for a highly skilled and educated citizenry. Change is the central theme in current educational planning.

School buildings should be the architectural expression of the educational programs they are designed to serve. Therefore, long-term planning of educational facilities should take a long, incisive look at emerging changes in educational programs. One of three alternatives must be selected: (1) reject or ignore the new concept; (2) accept or utilize the new concept in planning future school buildings; or (3) plan the buildings so they may be easily modified to permit implementation of a new concept at some later date. Each concept must be succinctly defined and the architect must know which of the three alternatives has been selected by the educational planners.

A successful school building program requires the participation of many persons, the careful coordination and scheduling of a great diversity of activities, and sufficient time to plan carefully and execute the program. Economy, in the wise use of each tax dollar, is of vital importance. Economy, properly defined, means achieving the maximum return on each dollar. It should not be confused with cheapness resulting in high maintenance costs, or early obsolescence of a school building, or the omission of needed educational spaces. It should also be noted that planning new school buildings can and should serve as the "triggering" device for the improvement of existing educational programs.

A Changing Curriculum

The most significant single trend in planning modern educational facilities has been the rapid modification in techniques of planning. During past decades, school buildings were constructed with little attention given to changing trends in the educational program. Upon completion, attempts were made to fit the existing and future curriculum into the building perimeter. In fact many school buildings of recent vintage are already educationally obsolete because of this planning method.

It can be said with certainty that tomorrow's educational planners will be primarily curriculum specialists, with new school construction serving as "prime mover" to the improvement of educational programs and the expansion of educational services. This curriculum-centered planning has already resulted in flexibility and expansibility being two of the most common characteristics of recent school buildings.

To aid the planners of future educational facilities, a summary of some of the major emerging educational concepts are listed:

1. Large Group Instruction
2. Small Group Seminars
3. Independent Study
4. Team teaching
5. Individualized Programs
6. Ungraded Instruction
7. Variable Time Blocks
8. Professional and Nonprofessional Staffing
9. Electronic Learning Aids
10. Instructional Materials Center
11. Language Laboratories
12. Programmed Learning
13. Schools-within-a School
14. Informal Learning and Counseling Areas
15. Teacher Planning Areas
16. Expanded and Changing Vocational-Technical Programs
17. Continuing Curriculum Change

This partial list is presented to illustrate that education is in a period of rapid change. All future planning should carefully consider these and other emerging concepts.

Implications for Educational Facilities

Most existing school buildings do not lend themselves to emerging educational programs. In fact, it is expensive, difficult, and sometimes impossible to convert an overaged school building to such educational concepts as large group instruction, small group seminars, and instructional materials centers. Unfortunately the above statement is also true of most schools planned during recent years and some buildings being planned today. The planner should recognize that the educational facility being planned today must be designed to serve well into the twenty-first century. To illustrate the implications of emerging educational concepts on educational facilities, a few of the concepts are analyzed.

Team teaching. There are many possible ways of organizing teachers into teams designed to efficiently utilize the unique and differing strengths and skills of each teacher. But all the methods now being tried in experimental team teaching programs are severely handicapped when forced to function in a typical school building—two rows of classrooms of equal size separated by a long narrow corridor.

Team teaching programs all appear to require school space that provides several fundamental principles not available in many schools today:

1. The space must be able to accommodate groups of various sizes, anywhere from 100 students down to one or two children studying by themselves.
2. The space must allow the rapid shifting of group size and the rapid changing of the participants of any group—continual motion throughout the school day is one inevitable result of team teaching.
3. The space should include a place where teachers can meet and work privately and, hopefully, a workroom for the preparation of special instructional material.[1]

---

[1] *Schools for Team Teaching* (New York: Educational Facilities Laboratories, Inc., 1961), p. 12.

Independent study.   Some school districts have adopted independent study programs in a futile attempt to save money. Actually this term should be entitled "guided independent study," and when done correctly it requires more teacher time, more space, and more money. It is founded on the basic premise that education is designed to assist each student in becoming self-educating; that each individual's needs, interests, and abilities are uniquely different from his peers; and that space and professional guidance should be provided for these purposes. Independent study carrels, programmed learning areas, and informal decentralized library spaces are examples of spaces being provided for independent study. Careful planning may frequently recapture poorly utilized areas of the building and convert these spaces to independent study purposes.

Instructional materials center.   The older concept of converting a classroom or two into a book storage room (library) is being replaced by the expanded idea of an instructional materials center. Electronic teaching-learning aids, individual study carrels, small group spaces, audiovisual centers, programmed learning areas, and the library are being integrated into one coordinated complex serving as the "nerve-center" of the school. In fact, a few schools are moving toward as much as 50 per cent of the school building being designed as "library-like" research and study space. Electronic central storage and retrieval systems are making it possible to bring any formalized information to a student when he needs the materials. It may be possible in a few short years to have a national or regional storage and retrieval system of video-tapes, slides, films, microfilms, records, filmstrips, and other materials. This instructional materials center could be relayed to states, educational institutions, libraries, and homes. The student would consult a directory or professional consultant, select the material needed, and dial the material to be seen and heard via a TV screen and speaker. A few educational institutions are already providing this service to students on a local and limited basis.

The Planning of Change

Much time, thought, and writing has been devoted to the planning of changes in educational programs and resultant school buildings. Little attention, however, has been given to how effectively and efficiently these new school buildings are being utilized. The writer recently has had the opportunity of visiting a large number of new school buildings located throughout the United States. Schools visited were selected from those schools that had instituted new ideas in school programs and design. Several observations were made:

1. Changes imposed by an outside individual or agency on the teaching staff tended to disappear within a few years.
2. Little relationship exists between the written reports of change in the school and the actual amount of change noted.
3. There appears to be a greater propensity for change in New England and the West than was observed in the Midwest and South.
4. Change in programs and facilities, contrary to some writers, was costing more money than traditional programs and was being done for the improvement of education and not for the purpose of reducing expenditures.
5. Changes, which were continuing in use, were preceded by inservice programs for teachers and a public information program for citizens and students.
6. "Crash" programs of new design were frequently poorly planned and difficult to utilize.
7. Most changes were found in suburban school districts and not in rural or large city school districts. A few notable exceptions were found in several large cities.
8. A surprising amount of change may be found in most new school buildings.
9. Change is a continuous process with many initial educational changes being frequently modified and adapted to make them more workable.
10. The question permeating most new school design was not, "Should we design for change?" but rather, "What changes should be provided?"

A Case Study

When initiating the educational planning of future school buildings, local planning committees frequently visit selected new school buildings. These educational facilities are usually selected because they have utilized a large number of emerging curriculum or architectural innovations. It is interesting to note the typical reaction of these visiting committees. Usually they discover that there are many problems resulting from the incorporation of these changes. Some of the planned educational changes have already been modified or rejected by the staff of the new school. The visitors are appalled by the apparent lack of measurable success of many of the new concepts.

They then proceed to plan a school quite different from the building they had previously envisioned. Visitations and analysis of selected new school plants appears to be one effective method of speeding the process of change.

This section of the chapter presents a composite case study of several new elementary schools recently constructed. This description is designed to assist the reader in the educational planning of future school buildings. It is not proposed as an ideal or final answer but rather to serve as a stimulant for discussion and evaluation prior to developing educational specifications for future school buildings.

The planning process.   The planning team consisted of a large number of human resources available to the school district. All had differing roles and changing responsibilities as the planning progressed. The planning team was directed by the school principal and included volunteer members of the school's teaching, clerical, and custodial staff. Selected lay citizens and students were added to the planning team. The school architect was employed early in the initial educational planning stage and served as a key resource person to the group. An educational consultant in planning educational facilities and curriculum specialists were added to the team. One year was budgeted for educational planning prior to the development of the architect's plans and specifications. The work of the planning team culminated in the development of written educational specifications designed to guide the architect in the architectural planning of the school building.

Curriculum planning was the team's first order of business. The existing educational program was carefully evaluated through the use of "self-study" materials. Emerging innovations in education were identified, evaluated, and considered for use in the new school.[2] Recent research findings about teaching and learning were reviewed by the group.[3] It is important to note that the board of education provided the team with time for planning, financial assistance, and specialized consultants. The end product of this planning procedure was as follows:

1. An intensive period of long-term curriculum planning.
2. A continuing in-service program designed to aid the teaching

---

[2] See page 96 for a partial listing of these concepts.
[3] "What Research Says About Teaching and Learning," *Phi Delta Kappan*, Vol. XXXIX, No. 6 (March 1958), 242–284.

staff in the implementation and evaluation of emerging curriculum concepts (i.e., the ungraded primary school, team teaching, electronic teaching aids, a modern mathematics program, etc.).

3. A new school building designed for use and easy adaptation to emerging and future curriculum changes.

Perhaps the most significant result of this cooperative planning process is the fact that the building is quite different from the staff's original concept of the new school; yet these new concepts have a far greater chance of acceptance and proper use because of the staff's careful involvement in the educational planning of their new school. Historically, imposed change has little likelihood of acceptance or success when autocratically thrust upon a teaching staff.

The teaching and custodial staff also served as valuable aids to the architect in suggesting improvements to his preliminary plans, detailed layouts of various areas, and final working drawings and specifications.

The school site.   A fifteen-acre site was purchased to serve as a combination school-park-neighborhood center. The site was selected well in advance of actual needs and is located in the approximate center of a developing residential neighborhood. The homes are within a half-mile radius of the school with the children walking inward through residential streets and away from commercial-industrial areas and dangerous major traffic arteries. Bus transportation costs, along with the expense of building pedestrian overpasses or providing stoplights and crossing guards were avoided. The site was selected, purchased, and developed in cooperation with the City Planning Commission, the Department of Parks and Recreation, the City Public Library, and other related governmental and civic organizations.

A prime consideration in the selection of the site was the area's natural beauty—rolling acreage forested with evergreens and hardwoods. The site's aesthetic qualities were preserved and enhanced by careful planning. The foliage was skillfully "manicured" and the buildings were planned to blend with its terrain and woods. The hilly site was not cleared and flattened as is frequently the case. A small stream flowing through one corner of the site was retained and its lower portion dammed to provide a shallow all-year pond.

This site is considered as serving a vital portion of the teaching-learning process, with the parents, teachers, and children contributing to its continuous change and improvement. For example, a community project designed to create a bird sanctuary on the site is currently under consideration. A small ravine was developed as an outdoor amphitheatre to serve the school-community. One small corner of the site is designated a "senior-citizens" area with appropriate facilities to serve this increasingly important segment of our society. Tables designed to serve as combination outdoor work spaces and picnic facilities have been provided by a civic organization. The school-park concept has been utilized in the planning of properly related building facilities and outdoor recreational areas. Decentralized play spaces of differing sizes have been provided for the kindergarten children, the primary grades, and the upper grades. Service facilities and adequate parking spaces are separated from the play areas.

It is interesting to note the economic considerations involved in this site. Long-range cooperative planning resulted in early acquisition of a large and properly located site at a reasonable cost. Expensive transportation costs were avoided. Creative site planning avoided large expenditures for leveling, grading, filling, and clearing of a rolling wooded site. Site acquisition and development costs were shared with the Park Board. This site will, obviously, contribute to increasing the property value of the residential community it serves.

The total building complex. Three separate "little-schools" are clustered around a central instructional-services building. The single-story school plant is located on the higher elevations of the site and is blended into the rolling tree-covered terrain. The building lines are low, simple, and uncluttered. Interior and exterior spaces are joined by the utilization of compatible building materials, building scale, and the use of an extended roof overhang. The roof overhang also provides partial heat control, reduces sky-glare in the classrooms, and furnishes rainy-day outdoor play areas. The profusion of trees, grass, and other plantings creates a beautiful site while contributing to the improvement of the classroom visual-thermal-audio environment.

One important part of the written educational specifications developed by the planning team was the inclusion of a series of adjectives to describe to the architect the desired psychological mood to be created by the total school building and its various components.

Among the adjectives used were friendly, inviting, informal, non-threatening, gay, colorful, stimulating, child-scaled, natural, changeable, and unfinished. These adjectives also provided the educational planners with a partial criterion to aid in evaluating the architect's design solutions.

One central objective in planning was to establish beauty as an important value to be stressed in the teaching-learning process. Beautiful school buildings need not be costly nor does the achievement of aesthetic goals conflict with designing functional spaces. The resultant simplicity of design played a major role in achieving a superior school building at a reasonable cost.

The instructional services building. The central building was designed to serve each of the three "little-schools" with those specialized areas, teaching-learning materials, and professional specialists that cannot be efficiently and effectively decentralized. This area, connected to the "little-schools" by covered walkways, provides the following basic spaces: (1) administrative suite, (2) teacher-planning space, (3) instructional materials center, (4) large group activities room (multi-purpose space), and (5) custodial services.

The central theme of this building is to maximize instructional services and assistance to each classroom, teacher, and child. For example, the school principal was selected, trained, and designated as the school's instructional leader and her normal "housekeeping" chores are assigned to a secretary-administrative assistant. A full-time clerical assistant is employed to relieve the teaching staff of many of their nonprofessional tasks (duplicating instructional materials, scoring objective tests, recording data, filing, etc.).

The entrance to the instructional services building was designed to serve as an instructional space rather than a typical school lobby and corridor area. The adjectives friendly, inviting, informal, changeable, usable, and beautiful were used to guide the architect in designing this space. An outdoor Japanese garden was blended into this area by the use of an open plan combined with extensive use of exterior glass. Among the activities served by this space are: (1) science projects, including movable and changeable aquariums, terrariums, and a large floor-to-ceiling birdcage; (2) an art project display area; and (3) an informal small group planning area for community use. Coffee is readily available, and students, parents, teachers, and civic groups are encouraged to use the area. It should be noted that this space was deliberately left in an unfinished condition. Planters, informal furniture, carpeting, and other needed furniture and equipment is being planned and provided by students, parents, and community organizations. This area and the library have been designed for evening and holiday use without the necessity of opening, heating, and lighting other sections of the school.

The instructional materials center consists of a library, an audiovisual area, and a teaching-learning materials area. The library area may best be described as resembling the living room of a scholar. It is carpeted, contains small browsing areas with comfortable informal furniture, avoiding fixed rows of tables and chairs. Independent study carrels are located throughout the library. A small group conference room is also provided. This library area uses large expanses of glass to advertise and invite its extensive use. Sliding glass doors open into a secluded outdoor garden area. Movable "islands" of book shelving make it possible to change the shape and form of this instructional area.

The audiovisual area is interrelated to the library and contains space for preparation, previewing, minor repairs, and storage of a wide variety of audiovisual materials and equipment. It is designed so that equipment and materials may be easily moved to and from the classrooms without interfering with the library program. Connected to the audiovisual area is a teaching-learning materials area. A wide variety of teaching aids are cataloged, organized, and easily transported to the classrooms. The instructional materials center has been staffed to provide maximum service to the school. The librarian, for example, serves as a consultant to teachers, parents, and children and does not act as a guard, clerk, and repairman. She is provided with student assistants and a full-time clerical aid. Both the librarian and the clerical aid have been trained in the use of audiovisual materials. It should be noted that the instructional materials center has been planned for future expansion. In fact, one major goal of the planning team was to achieve a school in which as much as 50 per cent of the school was "library-like" in appearance and use.

The three "little-schools." The "little-school" concept has been developed in an attempt to combine the advantages of both large and small schools. The comprehensive facilities available to larger schools are provided in a centrally located building while small-school intimacy is achieved by the decentralization of small groups of students and teachers into little-schools. It should be noted that this concept may be achieved in both sprawling campus plans or in compact educational facilities.

The three little-schools consist of a kindergarten building, a primary school (Grades 1–3), and an intermediate school (Grades 4–6). The kindergarten may best be described as "home-like" and is designed to soften the child's initial psychological shock of leaving home and family and facing his first major environmental change. A two-teacher kindergarten has been combined into one open space and team-teaching is employed. One teacher may be working with a larger group in such activities as "story-time," large group musical activities, "show-and-tell," or "learning-games," while the other member of the team is helping an individual child, working with a small group engaged in a special project, conferring with a parent, or planning future activities. Parental participation in kindergarten activities is encouraged with the parents affectionately described as "slave-labor" members of the team. One large proportion of the kindergarten floor is covered with bright red carpeting of easily cleaned material. The kindergarten area has been planned with its own entrance and exit to an isolated outdoor play and study area. A "wet-area" with sinks, work space, and ceramic tile flooring occupies one portion of the room. All of the furniture, equipment, and play apparatus in the kindergarten area is both easily movable and replaceable. Several quiet areas may be provided in the kindergarten room by the rearrangement of the furniture. Large expanses of window areas have been avoided in this room in order to reduce rapid heat gains and losses while making the room easily usable for a wide variety of audiovisual equipment.

The primary school and intermediate school each consists of ten classrooms clustered around a central "commons." This educational space (the commons) replaces the typical corridor area found in most traditional schools. The commons is designed for use as a large group instructional area as well as for providing space and equipment for group project work and independent study. Kilns, sinks, work counters, science equipment, and other specialized equipment are located around the perimeter of the commons. The commons opens visually into each of the ten classrooms through the use of extensive interior glass areas. Each classroom has movable drapes across these interior windows, giving the teacher the option of opening her classroom into the commons or classroom privacy. Her students may be working in either the classroom or in the commons area. Eight of the classrooms may be converted into four larger instructional areas by the use of easily movable partition walls. The planning of these little-schools provides the teaching staff with the opportunity and option of operating a traditional school program or of easily introducing emerging educational concepts such as large group instruction, team teaching, independent study, and small group seminars. It is significant to note that educational planners have long recognized individual differences in students while largely ignoring the inherent individual differences of the teaching staff. It is fallacious to assume that all teachers can operate most effectively utilizing identical teaching techniques. Some teachers operate most effectively as a member of a teaching team; most teachers require a combination of team teaching and individual classroom instructional activities. A few of our most able and creative teachers may be classified as "isolates" and cannot operate efficiently and effectively in a team situation. The school building should recognize these innate differences in both children and teachers and should provide space and environment easily adaptable to these unique differences. Lastly, the educational facilities should recognize continuing and rapid change as the single most important characteristic of our American society. The educational program and school building facilities serving this society must be easily adaptable to serve these continuing changes. School buildings being designed today will be in use for another half-century. Future educational changes should not be prohibited or restricted by a school building of an inflexible design.

Emerging School Buildings

Most new school buildings contain variations of many of the emerging educational concepts previously listed. Several other characteristics should be mentioned. Architects and manufacturers are providing increased freedom to the educational planner. For example, longer interior distances may now be spanned. The thermal, visual, and acoustical environment may be precisely controlled. Interior spaces are easily changeable and divisible into other uses. Buildings may be readily expanded. Beautiful school buildings are being provided while comparative costs are being reduced. All these improvements in school design may be largely credited to careful educational planning, creative architects, and our competitive economy.

Today and tomorrow represent exciting periods in the history of planning school buildings. The Conant report with its emphasis on a common core of general education for all, along with specialized opportunities,[4] the Trump report's emphasis on varying class sizes to meet the differing teaching-learning situations,[5] new technologies such as television, teaching machines, language laboratories, new methods of storing and retrieving information—these forces, and many more, insure the importance of creative planning of educational facilities. Throughout our nation space designers, curriculum designers, and interested lay citizens are planning school buildings designed to serve our rapidly changing world.

[4] James B. Conant, *The American High School Today* (New York: McGraw-Hill Book Company, 1959).

[5] Lloyd Trump, *Images of The Future* (Washington, D.C.: National Education Association, Department of Secondary School Principals, 1962).

Bibliography

American Association of School Administrators, *Planning American School Buildings*. Washington, D.C.: The Association, 1960.

Bursch, Charles W. and John Lyon Reid, *High Schools, Today and Tomorrow*. New York: Reinhold Publishing Corp., 1957.

Caudill, William W., *Toward Better School Design*. New York: F. W. Dodge Corporation, 1954.

Educational Facilities Laboratories, Inc., *The Cost of a Schoolhouse*. New York: The Laboratory, 1960.

————, *Profiles of Significant Schools*. New York: The Laboratory, 1959–1964.

Engelhardt, N. L., N. L. Engelhardt, Jr., and Stanton Engelhardt, *School Planning and Building Handbook*. New York: F. W. Dodge Corporation, 1956.

Herrick, John H., Ralph McLeary, Wilfred Clapp, and Walter Bogner, *From School Program to School Plant*. New York: Holt, Rinehart & Winston, Inc., 1956.

Leu, Donald J. and Richard L. Featherstone, *Room 103, Deployable Space*. East Lansing, Michigan: The College of Education, Michigan State University, 1963.

Leu, Donald J. and John L. Forbes, *What is Involved in Conducting a School Plant Survey?* East Lansing, Michigan: The College of Education, Michigan State University, 1956.

Leu, Donald J. and John J. McNicholas, *Planning for the Future*. Minneapolis, Minnesota: Minneapolis Board of Education, 1963.

MacConnell, James D., *Planning for School Buildings*. Englewood Cliffs, N.J.: Prentice-Hall, Inc., 1957.

McQuade, Walter, *Schoolhouse*. New York: Simon and Schuster, Inc., 1959.

National Council on Schoolhouse Construction, *Guide for Planning School Plants*, East Lansing, Michigan: The Council, 1964.

National Elementary Principals, *Elementary School Buildings—Design for Learning*. Washington, D.C.: National Education Association, 1959.

Perkins, Lawrence B., *Work Place for Learning*. New York: Reinhold Publishing Corp., 1957.

Strevell, Wallace H. and Arbid J. Burke, *Administration of the School Building Program*. New York: McGraw-Hill Book Company, 1959.

Sumption, Merle R. and Jack L. Landes, *Planning Functional School Buildings*. New York: Harper and Row, Publishers, 1957.

Index

Surety bond forms, 52
Surveys (*see* School plant studies)

T

Taxes, property, as a source of financing, 73
Teachers:
  differences in, 106
  needs of, 45
Team teaching, 97
Traffic arteries, 15, 16
Traffic map, 16
Trump report, 107

U

Urban redevelopment, 16, 17

U.S. Office of Education, report of school room shortage, 71

V

Ventilating system, 44
Virginia plan, 75

W

Washington matching plan, 75
Willis, Benjamin C., 4, 33
Wright, Frank Lloyd, 3

Z

Zoning, 14, 15